CASEY ROSS

Life & Faith

from "This is it?" to "This is it!"

First edition

ISBN: 979-8-9870965-0-5

Cover art by Christie Carey

This book was professionally typeset on Reedsy.
Find out more at reedsy.com

Contents

They Think You Should Read This Book

In *Life & Faith*, my friend Casey Ross provides readers with a clear and practical approach to following Jesus, which makes our lives better and makes us better at life. And it makes the lives of those around us better as well. Whether you're new to faith or a veteran Jesus follower, you will find *Life & Faith* a valuable resource.

Andy Stanley - Founder and Senior Pastor, North Point Ministries

I remember the first time I ever met Casey, I simply threw out the question "What is the best way to disciple people?" His eyes got big and a smile came over his face. He said, "I don't know the answer today, but I want to find out." Casey is a caring leader who loves to be in the messiness of people's lives and help them deepen their faith in Jesus. I can't wait for you to dive into his book!

Chris Emmitt - Senior Pastor, Local Church

Way too many people end up feeling like Christianity isn't exactly what they hoped for. Or is it? In this book, Casey Ross will help you rethink some key issues that can help you own your faith on a deeper level.

Carey Nieuwhof - Best Selling Author, Speaker, and Podcaster
Founder, The Art of Leadership Academy

This is it! The book that will challenge your perspective on your own role and the church's role in growing your faith. It's refreshing, raw, and just what the church needed.

Jeremy Cole – Lead Pastor, Mosaic Church Dubai (Dubai, United Arab Emirates)

We were called to live an abundant life. Casey Ross explains how to tap into an abundant faith-filled life that transcends present circumstances. Using his own experiences as a leader and pastor, Casey provides a path to finding or even rediscovering the joy and excitement of our daily walk with Christ.

Dee Ann Turner - Best Selling Author of *Bet on Talent* and *Crush Your Career*
Vice President, Chick-fil-A, Inc. (Retired)

I've known Casey for many years now and he has never settled. He keeps moving forward knowing with each step he's closer to "This is it!" The same is true for you and in this book he shows you how.

Jeff Henderson - Best Selling Author of *What to do Next*

This is it?! Many of us have felt that something was not quite right in our life. And too many of us have responded in very unhelpful ways to that feeling. In his new book, *Life & Faith,* my friend Casey Ross writes with humor and clarity about faith, humans, and the relatable yearning for more in this messy and beautiful thing called life. This book reminds us that life is a series of steps and at any point, you are bound to stumble and even fall. However, Casey offers helpful suggestions on how to confidently take the essential steps toward a life that does not disappoint you.

Chinwé Williams - Ph.D., Therapist, and Author

Casey's book is for anyone who has ever wondered, "This is it?" about their life and faith. You don't have to settle for disappointment. In his relatable style, Casey provides a practical way to experience life and faith in ways that make them hopeful and meaningful while benefiting those around you.

Clay Scroggins - Author of *How to Lead When You're Not in Charge*

The first time I saw Casey I recall a look on his face that seemed to ask, *This is it?* There wasn't the least hint of disrespect. It was genuine interest. Soon I saw a young man of perception and depth with a humble heart for service and an unwavering and attractive faith. That was more than three decades ago. Casey, now a husband and father who has served in strategic ministries across the Southeast, has taken that long ago *This is it?* and now declares *This is it!* His message is a good one, a wise one, a fun — and funny — one. But most of all, *Life & Faith* will take you from simply settling for a life of faith to seizing each day for Christ.

David Bennett - Managing Editor, Lifeway

I met Casey Ross in 2013 and immediately knew that I wanted to be his friend. It wasn't because of his stunning good looks or engaging personality, but because he was humble, funny, smart, and had something to say that was worth listening to. I recommend *Life & Faith* because Casey is worth listening to.

Jon Estes - Director and CEO, Woodlands Camp and Retreat Center

There is rarely a day that passes that I don't find myself applying a lesson learned from Casey Ross. Not only is he such a great people leader that I worked for him twice, but he is also a dad, husband, and pastor that leaves everyone better because they crossed his path. I have no doubt that this book will continue that trend of leaving people better because of Casey!

Ryan Fitzgerald - Senior Marketing Manager, BELAY Solutions

What I love most about *Life & Faith* is it is Casey, through and through. Casey Ross is a leader and writer who, using both personal stories and Scripture, walks you to the edge of a bottomless pool, the one you have only wished you had the guts to jump into, then dives in first, returning to the surface to tell you how great the water is! You can't help but want that kind of faith. Each chapter includes questions and suggestions for next steps, guiding the reader towards the "This is it!" life and faith we've all longed for. I loved it and look forward to going through it again, this time with a friend!

Kim Sanders - Wife, Mom, Mimi, and Founder of @nowmyeyeseesyou

In this book, Casey Ross has insightfully and vulnerably identified real issues at the heart of Western Christ-followers, and courageously challenged the status quo with authenticity, humility, and practicality. Whether you are a long-standing Christ-follower, or new to faith in Jesus, reading this book will encourage you to own your life and faith reality, and move forward with purpose and vibrancy. It will also leave feeling like you've made a great new friend."

Adam Low - Lead Pastor, Real Life Christian Church (Queensland, Australia)

All of us could use a little help placing more trust in Jesus. In his book, Casey encourages each of us to be more intentional in growing our faith by taking one more step.

Frank Bealer - Author of *The Myth of Balance*
Co-Founder, Phase Family Centers

I believe the best authors write a story using stories. That is exactly was Casey Ross has done with *Life & Faith*. Casey is a great writer, and an even better storyteller, which makes the reader feel like he or she is sitting down with the author and having a great conversation over a cup of coffee. In this day and time where we can all relate to having a complicated life, Casey draws the reader in and helps them see the struggles of life from a much needed Biblical perspective. I love this book, and I highly recommend it to all readers who want to be inspired to get the most out of their lives.

John Robison - Director of Public Safety, Alpharetta, Georgia

Consistently and appropriately connecting our lives with the faith we profess is challenging but vital. Casey Ross provides excellent guidance in his book *Life & Faith*. Drawing from wide experience in his own life and ministry, he gives reliable wisdom for overcoming the complications of faith and culture, taking the necessary steps to grow personal faith. We all want to leave a legacy of untarnished respect and purpose. For anyone serious about translating that hope into reality, this book will assist in coupling words and actions for a productive and satisfying life.

Dwight Mason - Lead Pastor, NewPointe Community Church
Author of *Only God*

I love meetings with my friend and co-worker Casey Ross. I know every meeting will include a good story or two, a laugh (usually at his expense), and some really great but practical advice or next steps. That's what his new book feels like! So many times in life, we either over-complicate things and are paralyzed to take the next step or we settle because we think things are okay when just one extra step can turn the okay into the great! I think his new book could be the next step that many of us need to take!

Mandi Holcombe - Next Gen Pastor, Local Church

I've been blessed to call Casey my boss, mentor, and, most importantly, friend. There are a few things you should know about him. He loves Jesus, Chick-fil-A, and people. In his book, *Life & Faith,* he recounts his personal experiences and shares how your next step could be one of the most important decisions of your entire life. You need to read this book!

Robbie Caesar - Director of Marketing: Operations, North American Mission Board

In this book, Casey addresses a topic everyone can relate to....no matter where they are in their faith journey. He does so with humor, honesty, and personal stories. Filled with practical tips and thought-provoking questions, this book will benefit anyone struggling with their faith or wanting to grow their faith.

Donna Vonfeldt - Mom, Grandmother, and Longtime Friend

This is a great read that is filled with many moments of laughing out loud while helping one to reflect deeply on their view of life. Casey's ability to connect with the reader through his personal stories facilitates needed introspection in a practical and accessible way that will leave you thankful and ready to implement his tangible insights.

Derrick Hershey - Educator

1

LIFE

You are different. You are unique. But...

You are more like everyone than you are different from everyone. You have so much in common with all people. That does not make you less special. I think it's an amazing, beautiful thing. All the things we have in common give us the ability to relate to each other and accomplish together.

I think one thing we have in common is feeling like, "This is it?" I don't know if you realize you feel this way, but most people do not live enjoyable, satisfying lives. You're just going through the motions. You may have a highlight every once in a while, but not that often. Deep down, you know life should be more. Can you relate? I can.

We will spend time together in the first five chapters looking at life. Specifically, how to live your life in a way that does not feel disappointing. And you don't have to fill up your calendar, spend more money, one-up your previous experience, or have a better life than someone else to have a fulfilling life.

I want you to live a life that feels like, "This is it!" It's not a perfect life. It's not a one-size-fits-all life. It's your life. It's a fulfilling life no matter what happens, and a lot is going to happen. I think life can be more than you've experienced and more than you've imagined.

2

SOMETHING'S NOT RIGHT

I 'll never forget that Thanksgiving. We spent a few days at the beach with my parents. We watched football. We ate too much. We played on the beach. And we just enjoyed being together. But something was not right about my dad.

My dad, aka "Pop," was a fantastic grandfather. He would play with our kids, cheer them on, engage them in conversations, and ask them meaningful questions. I loved watching him be a grandfather. He was a great dad too.

I couldn't quite figure out what was not right about him. He was himself most of the time, but sometimes, he was not himself. I think I did what most people would do: I explained the odd feeling away. I told myself I was reading into things, but that feeling just kept coming back.

I waited weeks before saying something to my mom and brother. I didn't want to believe anything was wrong with him. I did not want to be the first person to bring it up. What if I was wrong? What if they resented me for bringing it up? What if my dad found out what I said?

We'll never know when my dad's dementia started. At first, the disease slowly spread throughout his life. He'd be himself; then suddenly, it was like he was a different person. Eventually, the disease took over his whole body. Less than two years after that Thanksgiving, he died.

Do you ever get the feeling something is not right?

You may think it's the voice inside of you or your gut telling you something is not right. Maybe it's your intuition or discernment. Perhaps it's God. All you know is something is not right.

HOW DO YOU RESPOND WHEN SOMETHING FEELS NOT RIGHT?

As we left the beach that Thanksgiving, I felt like I had three options. It took me weeks to decide which option to choose. When I made the decision, I was unsure I'd made the right decision. Honestly, it was months before I felt confident I had made the right decision.

There are three ways to respond when you feel like something is not right.

IGNORE THE FEELING

You already know this, but this is what most people choose to do. It's the easiest choice. You feel like something is wrong. You think about it. You decide to ignore or minimize the feeling - and you move on.

If you pretend everything is okay, you don't have to deal with the problem. What problem? If there is nothing wrong, there is nothing to talk about. There is no work to be done. Dealing with the problem can be a lot of work. And think about all the what-ifs. What if others disagree with you? What if no one wants to help you? What if you're wrong?

It's always easiest to stay quiet. Hopefully, someone else will notice something is not right and do something about it. After all, you didn't create the problem. You just noticed it.

MAKE A BIG DEAL OUT OF THE FEELING

You have a feeling something is not right, but you're not sure what it is. Instead of ignoring it, you sound the alarm. You make sure everyone knows you feel like something is not right.

Do you know an escalator? I just made up that name. This is the person who escalates everything to level 10. Everything is a big deal, and everyone needs to know it is a big deal. Don't be this person. Eventually, this person is not trusted or believed because everything cannot be a big deal.

SAY SOMETHING ABOUT THE FEELING

There is a better way to respond when you feel like something is not right. You can say something. What is the right way to bring up what you're feeling?

- Be calm. You don't know if there is a problem. You just have a feeling something is not right.
- Be curious. Ask questions to understand the situation to determine if there is a problem.
- Be helpful. Make sure the person you're talking to knows you want to help no matter what.

YOU'RE RIGHT; SOMETHING IS NOT RIGHT

As you go through your day today, if you feel like something is not right, you're right. But it's probably not what you think it is. That feeling is not because of politics, social issues, health issues, or how someone is treating you. Those are symptoms of the real problem.

What is the real problem? **We live in a world that is not as it's meant to be.**

Genesis explains the real problem. After God created the world, Genesis 1:31 tells us, *"God saw all that he had made, and it was very good. And there was evening and morning – the sixth day."* And Genesis 2:25 says, *"Adam and his wife were both naked, and they felt no shame."*

God created our world just as He wanted it to be. He was pleased with it. It was good. As part of creation, he gave humans the ability to make choices. In Genesis 3:1-7, we read, *"Now the serpent was more crafty than any of the wild animals the Lord God had made. He said to the woman, "Did God really say, 'You must not eat from any tree in the garden'?"*

The woman said to the serpent, "We may eat fruit from the trees in the garden, but God did say, 'You must not eat fruit from the tree that is in the middle of the garden, and you must not touch it, or you will die.'"

"You will not certainly die," the serpent said to the woman. "For God knows that when you eat from it your eyes will be opened, and you will be like God, knowing good and evil."

When the woman saw that the fruit of the tree was good for food and pleasing to the eye, and also desirable for gaining wisdom, she took some and ate it. She also gave some to her husband, who was with her, and he ate it. Then the eyes of both of them were opened, and they realized they were naked; so they sewed fig leaves together and made coverings for themselves."

The world you live in changed the moment sin entered it. God created a perfect world. The first humans messed it up. The world was no longer as it was supposed to be. And you have to deal with it every day of your life.

That feeling that something is not right is like white noise in your life. Do you have noise in your bedroom that helps you sleep? Do you have noise in your office or house that enables you to block out other noises and focus?

You forget about white noise. You get used to it. It becomes normal. It's there in the background, just like that feeling you have that something is not right.

YOU CAN FEEL DIFFERENTLY

Even though you may not notice it daily, you know something is not right. Your mind, heart, and body feel it despite not consciously thinking about it. Your relationships are affected by it even if you're not aware of it. Even your faith, the most important thing about you, deals with it constantly. Every part of your life, even on the good days, is affected by the background noise that something is not right.

And a nagging sense of disappointment creeps into your life and faith. And you wonder, "This is it?"

You cannot fix the world we live in. This is not a problem to solve. It will always be not as it is supposed to be, but you can live in a way that causes you to feel differently about life. You can experience your faith in a way that causes you to feel differently about faith.

You can feel like, "This is it!" By the time you finish reading this book, I believe you can experience this kind of life and faith. It just takes one step.

ARE YOU FREE FOR LUNCH?

I'd prefer to sit across the table from you and talk about life and faith. I'm an introvert, but I like the back-and-forth of questions, answers, laughter, surprises, and stories. I'll share my experiences throughout the book. I hope it helps you connect with me a little better.

I became a pastor a year after I graduated college. I've worked in churches where you knew everyone's name and in churches larger than some cities. Jesus did not establish a country, a person, or a non-profit to carry his message around the world. He established the church to advance his message. I love working for and with the church.

I have seen some crazy stuff in my career - things you would not believe. There was the time the guy used "the force" on me. Yes, the Jedi Force from *Star Wars*. I am not kidding. I have not seen it all, but I have seen a lot.

My job gives me a front-row seat to peoples' lives. I've seen beautiful things and ugly things. I believe most people genuinely want to get life and faith right. I also think most people and churches are doing it wrong. I've done it wrong for a long time. We must do life and faith differently to experience life and faith differently. This book will help you do that.

The best part about me is my family. Julie and I met when we were in the 10th grade. It was love at first sight. Okay, that is not true. I thought she was hot. And she was popular and athletic. On top of that, she remembered my name. At that age, that's all I needed. She was clearly out of my league, but, of course, her acknowledging my existence gave me all the confidence I needed to ask her to see a movie with me...nine months after we met.

I actually like my three kids and want to spend time with them and talk to them. Let's assume they feel the same way about me.

You should also know I'm weird. I think all people are weird. I'm pretty aware of the many things that make me weird. Here are just a few:

- When I try on clothing and decide to buy an item, I purchase one I did not try on.
- I love to wear hoods – all the time.
- I won't use yellow highlighters.
- I visit Chick-fil-A about six times per week.
- I once made my family stalk an NFL Quarterback.

That's enough for now. I don't want to scare you away.

SINCE WE CAN'T DO LUNCH, I WROTE THIS

A couple of years ago, I took a step I thought I'd never take. I left my dream job at a dream church after 15 years of being a part of that organization. I went to work for a church in my community that I had not heard of until the day our friend posted on Instagram they were hiring. On my first day, I was given an assignment that bothered me the more and more I worked on it. As I worked on the project, what I learned and realized bothered me so much I had to do something about it. We changed how we did things at our church. And this book was born from that assignment. But this book is not about church. It's about you and me.

In the book's first five chapters, we will spend time together looking at life. Specifically, how to live your life in a fulfilling and not disappointing way. This truly can be your reality.

Why discuss life first? It's our common ground. We all experience life together. Let's start where our greatest needs are. We could discuss faith first, but if life feels too full and complicated, you will continue to separate faith from the rest of your life.

In the rest of the book, we will spend time together looking at faith. Specifically, how to experience your faith in a way that does not feel disappointing. Yes, it's okay to admit your faith feels disappointing. But it's not supposed to feel this way.

Since we cannot sit down and have this conversation, I put "Conversation Questions" at the end of each chapter. This book will be better and more helpful if you read it and discuss it with someone. Isn't just about everything better when you include others in it? We're a family of introverts, and even we know this. Walk through this book with a friend, accountability partner, small group, spouse, Bible study group, book club...you get the point. Your life and faith will improve even more if you read this book with others.

CONVERSATION QUESTIONS

Have you ever felt like something was not right, and you were correct? What was it?

When you feel like something is not right, which one of the three options is your typical response?

Right now, how are you most aware the world is not as it is supposed to be?

What do you do that makes you weird?

When do you feel like "This is it?" with your life and faith?

3

YOUR COMPLICATED LIFE

Julie and I met after a high school football game during the fall of 10th grade. It was not love at first sight. I don't think she could even see me. My friend Rhett was driving and I was in the front passenger seat. Julie sat directly behind me. Our friend Lara sat behind Rhett. We were in the car together for a total of maybe five minutes. We dropped Julie and Lara off at Burger King and drove away.

We didn't see each other again until that summer when we went to the same camp. It wasn't love at first sight then, either. But it was "she's hot" at first sight. Somehow, I found the courage to ask her to see Batman with me. And for some reason I will never understand, she said, "Yes." If you're wondering, Michael Keaton played Batman.

We attended the same college. Shout out to Presbyterian College! Go, Blue Hose! Weirdest mascot ever. We got engaged the summer before our senior year. We got married six weeks after we graduated college, and now we have three kids. Nothing but rainbows, unicorns, and glitter.

Well, not quite. Yes, everything above is true, but I left out some things. (And I hate glitter.) I thought about making a list of all the bad things that happened to us since the 11th grade, but that would be a big downer. So, I'll tell you about just one of those times. Actually, it was not a single moment in time. It was years of our lives.

Julie and I had a plan. I'd finish my master's degree; then we'd get "real" jobs, buy a house, and have our first kid. We'd live happily ever after. Those things happened just like they were supposed to, except for the part about us having a kid. It's fun trying to get pregnant, so we did not think much about it at first. But after a full year of not getting pregnant, we knew we needed to ask some questions.

Julie talked to some doctors about our situation, and there did not seem to be any issues. Great news! To check the box, I went to see a doctor too. I'll never forget that day.

As the doctor and I were wrapping up, he looked at me and said, "You're not going to be able to have kids without help from doctors. And you're the problem." Thank you for the excellent bedside manner. He said other things, but I didn't hear anything after that. I remember finishing up and asking him where the restroom was. I just stood in the restroom until the room stopped spinning. It took a while.

Julie was waiting for me in the car. It took me a few minutes to tell her what he'd said. She didn't believe me at first. The drive up Highway 277 was silent. We were both stunned. That is not what we'd expected. Our life just got way more complicated.

We went through years of infertility procedures, waiting, and consistent bad news that Julie was not pregnant. Then, amazingly, Julie got pregnant through in vitro fertilization (IVF.) We had our daughter!

IVF worked for us, so we did it again. And it worked again! We were on a roll! Then Julie had a miscarriage. A miscarriage is always terrible. For a couple dealing with infertility, it shattered us. We tried IVF again, and we had nothing to show for it. Well, we had something to show for it. We had tens of thousands of dollars in debt we now had to pay off.

We found out Julie was pregnant with our son six years after our daughter was born. And three years after that, we had another son. I have never been more surprised in my life. Our sons were the result of "the old-fashioned way" of getting pregnant – a lot cheaper and way more fun than IVF.

While we went through the rollercoaster of infertility, life around us continued. The jobs we had were meaningful. The friendships around us were beautiful. So many good things happened while we were visiting the doctors and getting bad news.

I don't believe in the "good old days." I know some people do. Some people want to go back to those days. But I can't figure out what days they're talking about. It seems they've made up some dreamy period that did not genuinely exist, or they had a good run of positive days but didn't realize others were suffering during that same time. The "good old days" to you were not the "good old days" to others.

I also don't believe life sucks. I've experienced too many good days to think that, but there have been times when I thought life sucked that day.

I hope you've had more good days than bad days, but I know you've had both. Parts of life are good. Some are even great. And parts of life are bad. Some are even terrible.

Sometimes it is one or the other. It's all good or all bad.

Often, though, the good and the bad happen at the same time.

Life is complicated that way. And complicated is not a bad thing. The word "complicated" means:

1: consisting of parts intricately combined
2: difficult to analyze, understand, or explain[1]

Life has always been complicated. We live in a world that is not as it was meant to be.

Jesus was constantly honest even when people did not like what he said. In John 16:33, he said, *"In this world you will have trouble."* You are going to experience trouble. Wasn't Jesus supposed to fix all your troubles? No. He came to save you from your troubles, but not how you'd expect him to.

I am convinced there is an answer to this complicated life we all experience. It's not a solution. This is not a problem that can be solved, but there is a way to be better at living this complicated life. You can manage the tension this life causes you to feel. We'll get to that soon.

HOW DO YOU KNOW LIFE IS COMPLICATED?

You can see complicated. You can hear complicated. You can even taste complicated. Ever had a Mexican pizza? So good! But it is "difficult to analyze, understand, or explain" because it consists of "parts intricately combined."

Even though life is complicated, you often get numb to it. You don't even realize how complicated it is for yourself or others. Life is made up of so many parts. And life is so difficult to explain even to ourselves. Yet, you often don't notice how complicated life is around you. You're desensitized to it all until it hits you like a lightning bolt.

You feel it even when you don't notice how complicated your life is. Your mind and body tell you how complicated life is. Here are some ways your mind and body alert you when life is complicated.

STRESS

Sometimes my kids tell me they're "stressed out," and I laugh. Sometimes I even remember not to laugh out loud. These are not my best parenting moments.

How can they feel stressed? They don't have a mortgage, college tuition payments, medical bills, a job, or three kids. I know what stress is! They have it easy.

And then I wake up and realize they feel stressed. We all feel stressed. And we all feel it for different reasons, at different times, and in different ways. A toddler can feel stress. A rich person can feel stress. A senior citizen can feel stress. You feel stressed when you feel overwhelmed by what is happening around you.

SHAME

Shame is dangerous. It can take you out. Don't confuse it with guilt. Guilt tells you that you did something you should not have done and must make it right. "Shame is the intensely painful feeling or experience of believing we are flawed and therefore unworthy of acceptance and belonging."[2]

Shame affects our identity. Shame does not say you did something bad. Shame says you are a bad person. You feel like you do not deserve love and acceptance from others. You feel alone. That is a frightening place to find yourself.

From me to you: you deserve love and acceptance no matter what you have done or said.

ANGER

What makes you angry? Why do those things make you angry?

I have some serious issues that anger me. And I have some petty things that anger me. Can you relate?

When you feel angry, your body tells you someone has been wronged. Often, that "someone" is you. A complicated life is filled with wrong things happening to you and others. Sometimes those wrong things are intentionally done, and others are unintentionally done. It doesn't matter. When you or someone else is wronged, you feel anger.

UNFAIRNESS

Life should be fair. Good things happen to good people. Bad things happen to bad people. And life would be as it should be. But life is not as it should be. Life is not fair.

We think bad people should get what they deserve, even if we don't say it out loud. However, they often get what the good people deserve - more money, more stuff, more access.

Children get cancer. People who do bad things get rich. My dad got dementia. I did not get the same body type as my brother. You didn't get that parking spot.

It's debatable how good I am. And, trust me, it has been debated. I broke up with Julie twice in college - our freshman year on her birthday. And again, our sophomore year on her birthday. Yes, I know I was a jerk. Keyword: "was." And, yes, people still remind me about this every year when her birthday happens. For the record: we are still together. In college, I walked in on people discussing how not good I was. That was weird. But my wife Julie is a unanimous good person. Just ask anyone who has ever known her. It's crazy.

Even our kids think she's fantastic. She recently won "best teacher" in the county we live in. Out of 6,000 plus teachers in all grades and all schools, she's the best. That is one vote I agree with 100%.

But Julie has battled anxiety and depression at different times. And our years of dealing with infertility were rough on her. We even went through a season when I had to give her injections in her butt. No one is bad enough to deserve that. Don't worry, though; I practiced on an orange. Seriously, I did. Life is not fair.

ANXIETY

My friend, Dr. Chinwé Williams, is a rock star therapist and author. She defines anxiety as a sense of uneasiness, nervousness, worry, or dread of what's about to happen or what might happen. Anxiety causes physical changes like an increased heart rate, increased blood pressure, or rapid breathing.[3]

If the future were clear, positive, and safe, we would rarely experience anxiety. But your life and the future are complicated, and anxiety is often the result.

The Ross family has a lot of experience with anxiety. Sometimes the reason for the anxiety is apparent. Other times, there appears to be no reason for it. It's complicated.

DISAPPOINTMENT

A complicated life feels disappointing. You consciously or subconsciously ask yourself, "This is it?" You know life should be better and different - and it is sometimes - but not all the time. Feeling unsatisfied, sad, and discouraged seems to sneak into your mind and emotions.

Can you relate to any of these signals that life is complicated? I can. There are more signals. Ever feel defeated? Ever feel out of control? Ever feel a lack of peace? More signs life is complicated. It's all around us.

WHAT (AND WHO) COMPLICATES LIFE?

Life has a natural drift to it. The drift is toward complexity. Life never naturally drifts you toward easy and simple. Think about your Homeowner's Association, business, or family. If left alone, they will drift toward more complicated.

You cannot help this natural drift. You can only choose to fight against it. And before you can fight against a complicated life, you must know what (or who) causes complications in your life.

OTHER PEOPLE

This is whom we blame most for our complicated life. Them. Him. Her. They. You know who complicates your life the most.

People say things they should not say and do things they should not do. And the consequences of those words and actions affect you. This is the understatement of the year.

You could share story after story of ways other people (strangers and people you know) have complicated your life. Other people have hurt your family members. Other people have caused damage to your property. Other people have caused you to be late. Other people have caused you pain. Other people have hurt you emotionally. Other people have abused you.

YOUR EXPECTATIONS

My friend Jon Estes leads the country's best camp for kids and students. Woodlands Camp just happens to be an hour from our house. All of our kids have participated in it, and my daughter worked there. He talks to the staff at the start of each summer about expectations. He teaches them, "The spirit of expectation is not your friend."

I hate that statement...because he's right. I struggle with high expectations. Your expectations are your desires for specific things to happen in the future. Sounds innocent. However, when those expectations are not met, you typically go to a bad place about that situation, person, or place that did not do what you wanted it to do. If you allow your unmet expectations to determine how you feel about someone or something, you're making life more complicated than it has to be.

SOCIAL MEDIA

Social media connects you to others and helps relationships go further and faster. Social media also stirs up comparison and envy. It's funny how the same thing can cause very different outcomes.

The photos and videos you post complicate life. Did you know that? Have you ever considered how much effort you put into posting the "right" image and the "right" words? I'm not saying you lie when you post. I'm just saying you put a lot of work into looking and sounding a certain way. And that complicates things for yourself and others.

HEALTH

Your health and the health of others complicate life. If you have not experienced this yet, just wait.

My dad died in his mid-seventies from dementia. He battled it for a few years, but we knew the outcome as soon as we heard the diagnosis. Dementia is an automatic death sentence with a terrible path between the diagnosis and the end. His health complicated his life, but the longer he suffered, the less he realized it. Dementia affected our whole family; the longer he suffered through it, the more complicated our lives became.

My friend Jason was diagnosed with dementia in his early forties. It's one thing for a senior citizen to get this disease, but it's another for someone in the middle of life to get it. His health affects the lives of his wife, three daughters, his in-laws, and his mom. And something this cruel at that stage of life is not fair.

YOU

Time for a reality check. Sit down or hold onto something secure. You cause most of the complications in your life, not other people. You. You are the common denominator in all the complications in your life.

When you don't fight the natural drift toward complexity, you cause and allow complexity in your life. You cause complications in others' lives, whether you mean to or not. Your words and actions create complications for you and many others.

It's just easier to blame everyone and everything else. It's easier if "they" cause our complications. It takes responsibility from you and gives it to someone or something else you cannot control.

THE RESULT OF A COMPLICATED LIFE

Have you ever been in the water (ocean, swimming pool, river, lake, etc.) and extended your legs downward so you could plant your feet on the bottom, only to find that your feet did not touch the ground? There was nothing. Your feet just continued to reach for something that was not there.

It's a frightening feeling when you cannot touch the bottom. What you thought was there is not there. Nothing is there. You're in the deep end. You search for anything that can provide the stability and safety you're looking for, but your feet touch nothing.

The result of a complicated life is the feeling of being in the deep end and unable to touch the bottom. You're looking for anything to plant your feet on firmly, but nothing is there. You're left desperate for anything that resembles the shallow end where you can place your feet on the ground.

We value shallow water. Our goal is to live in the shallow end. We desire to live a life that is the opposite of complicated. Easy and clear are our dreams, but they're just that - dreams. You can have moments of ease and clarity, but other people, expectations, social media, health, and you (and so many other factors) do not allow them to last forever. Eventually, the shallow end fills with water, and you cannot touch the bottom. That's life for us all.

ISN'T IT IRONIC?

I heard Ron Howard claim television and movies have not changed over the decades. I laughed and thought, "That's exactly what an old guy would say." Have you watched a television show from the 1970s lately? Even I laugh at those shows. Those shows are nowhere close to anything on a screen today.

Then I remembered who Ron Howard is. He's been acting, writing, and directing television and movies for more decades than I've been alive. His list of projects is in the hundreds, and I feel confident you've watched something he was a part of. I have acted in, written, and directed exactly zero television shows or movies. He may know more about this than I do.

Despite the tremendous advances in technology and processes, he says television and movies are still "breaking moments down, understanding them, recording them, and presenting them."[4] Okay. Good point. He's right.

Remember the definition of complicated?

1: consisting of parts intricately combined
2: difficult to analyze, understand, or explain

Life is complicated. What are the parts of life that are intricately combined? Work, family, friends, your past, emotions, goals, hobbies, health, etc. When all these parts blend together, your life becomes difficult to analyze, understand, or explain.

As complicated as life is, I believe there are two basic components to every part of your life: your words and your actions. Some of us say more words and do fewer actions. Others of us say fewer words and do more actions. But your complicated life is just some talking and some doing. Isn't it ironic?

NOW WHAT?

Your life is complicated, and so is the life of your best friend, the person who hurt you, the person you don't want to be in the same room with, the person you look up to, and every stranger you see. Some people hide it well. Some people put it on display for everyone to see.

Acknowledging life is complicated hopefully helps you cut yourself some slack. Your life is difficult. It is normal to feel stress, anxiety, fear, etc. When you take a deep breath and admit life is hard, taking steps to get better at life is more manageable.

Acknowledging life is complicated hopefully helps you cut others some slack, as well. I don't know what you have against them or what they did to you, but their life is complicated too. It doesn't excuse what they did, but it may help you loosen your grip around their neck.

To be better at life, we must move forward. We must live well in this complicated life. To live well, it helps to understand life can be broken down into two basic elements: words and actions.

CONVERSATION QUESTIONS

How does life feel complicated right now?

When do you feel like you're in the deep end and cannot touch the bottom?

Who/what most complicates your life?

How do you complicate your own life?

4

YOUR WORDS

I played soccer before it was cool to play soccer. It is cool now, right? When I was in middle school, we were playing another club team coached by Coach Hendricks. I played right defender, so it was common for me to be near the opponent's bench. I will never forget when he said to his striker, "You can beat him; he's fat." He was talking about me. I wasn't fat. I wasn't skinny either. It was his way of motivating his player, but I heard those words. And decades later, I remember his name. I remember the game was at East Riverside Park. I still feel something when I think about that time.

In elementary school, the kids in our neighborhood played a game in a concrete ditch two houses down from my house. The older kid I was competing against in some made-up game got mad at me and, without warning, shoved me down so that my forehead hit the brick wall lining the ditch. Yes, the result was lots of blood. My mom raced me to the doctor so I could get stitches. You know what? I don't remember the kid's name. I don't remember what game we were playing. And I honestly feel no emotion about it. It's just something that happened when I was a kid.

One guy physically hurt me and caused me to get stitches. One guy said something untrue about me to someone else. I feel nothing and don't remember any details about one. I feel something and remember lots of details about the other. Weird.

By the way, because I know you're wondering, I also remember I had a great game, shut down his attackers, and we won the game. His words motivated me more than his players. I played hundreds of soccer matches growing up. Why do I remember this specific one? Words. We have an interesting relationship with words.

THE POWER OF WORDS

My friend, author, speaker, and counselor Kathleen Edelman wrote a book called *I Said This You Heard That*. I cannot recommend this book enough. It forever changed our family and me for the better. Her life's mission is to help people use words that support and build others up. She wrote:

"For better and, unfortunately, for worse, the words you say and the words you hear have the power to shape your entire life. Your words have the power to shape other people's lives too."[5]

She always points people to a verse in the Bible written by Paul in a letter to some people who were trying to follow Jesus in a complicated world. He wrote in Ephesians 4:29, *"Do not let any unwholesome talk come out of your mouths, but only what is helpful for building others up according to their needs, that it may benefit those who listen."*

Would you be different if your parents, teachers, coaches, friends, siblings, etc., only said words that built you up and benefited you? Of course, you would be different!

You choose the words you say. Words can create:

- lifelong friendships
- romantic relationships
- enemies
- war
- peace
- understanding
- confusion
- intimacy
- division

Put certain words together, and you can make someone laugh so hard they cry. <Insert your favorite joke.>

Put certain words together, and you can damage someone for a lifetime. <Insert that thing someone said to you when you were younger.>

Put certain words together, and you can move people to do just about anything. <Insert the most significant movements the world has ever seen.>

Put certain words together, and you can cause people to feel emotions they did not know were inside them. <Insert the story that gets you every time.>

THE POWER OF SILENCE

My dad said you should never talk about three things: money, politics, and religion. His dad told him that. He believed even bringing up those topics would cause problems.

When we were about to move to Georgia, my dad wanted to "do lunch" because he said he wanted to apologize for something. My dad never wanted to "do lunch" in my entire life. My mind raced to some weird places. What did he want to apologize for? His other family in Idaho? The body he had hidden in the woods? How he faked his death to escape from the mob? His true identity as an assassin? I watch too many documentaries.

I made him "do lunch" ASAP. And I made him apologize ASAP. I was so relieved, but I could not believe what he apologized for. I thought he was joking. He apologized for not being involved in the faith part of my life when I was growing up. I was a pastor. I'd been one for years. When he finished apologizing, I exhaled in relief. Then I told him he was off the hook. People gave him credit for doing a great job in the faith part of my life. I'm a pastor.

He didn't care about any credit people gave him. He knew he'd not spoken into my faith when I was growing up. He was right. He regretted that for decades.

Silence about the topic of faith was my dad's greatest regret in our relationship.

THAT WORD

Words matter so much. There are words you cannot stand to say or hear. "That" word can cause you just to lose it.

Harry Potter is one of my favorite people...I mean characters of all time. (Yes, call me a nerd. By the way, I'd be in Slytherin. No surprise if you know me.) In the stories, he challenged a whole society by saying the word no one else would say. Saying the name of the evil villain had become forbidden. His name, just one word, was so feared that it held power over the good guys. Everyone called him "he who must not be named" or "you know who."

But Harry knew fear could only be overcome if they said his name. So, he would openly say his name: "Voldemort." Spoiler alert! Saying that word led to a revolution where the good guys eventually won!

The Boston Red Sox is a major league baseball team. Their fans have a word that elicits negative emotions and cuss words. I know it's "curse," but I am from South Carolina and live in Georgia. Just say "Yankees" around a Sox fan and see what happens. If they're true Sox fans, they will fire off some strong words you should not say in front of your mother. Their voices will get louder, and their faces will get redder as they show off that wicked Boston accent.

Are you familiar with the rivalry between The Ohio State University Buckeyes and the University of Michigan Wolverines football teams? Putting it lightly, they hate each other. Ohio State hates the word "Michigan" so badly that during the week before they play each other, it removes the letter "m" from every sign, social media post, etc., around the campus.

Ohio State hates the word "Michigan" 51 weeks out of the year. But for one week each year, they delete the starting letter of the word from their vocabulary. They create nonwords because they hate a word so badly. Is "nonword" even a word?

Words make us do crazy things.

Do you have a word that just drives you crazy? Maybe a word that makes you want to throw something or throw up?

Dictionary.com lists[6] the following words as some of the most hated words in the English language:

- moist
- mucus
- clogged
- slacks
- phlegm
- rural

Sorry if one of those triggered you. Sorry if the word "trigger" triggers you.

My daughter hates the word "moist." Many people do. It shows up in almost every Google search for "most hated words."

Unfortunately for my daughter, she has two younger brothers. And they are pros at doing what brothers do best: bothering their sister. It's probably why that word does not bother me. I've heard my sons work "moist" into so many conversations with her just to get a reaction from her. I'm numb to the word now.

Moist. Moist. Moist. See, it doesn't bother me.

LIFE IS TALKING

Some of us talk more. And some of us talk less. Where we are, who we are, or who we're with plays into how much we talk. But we all talk.

When I was a kid, I made my grandmother cry because she worried about how shy I was and how little I talked. Now there are times when even I wish I would shut up.

Your words are interesting.

You say things you should not say. And you regret it.

You regret not saying things you should say.

You intentionally say words you know you should not say.

One of my favorite things as a pastor is when someone cusses or almost cusses around me. If they almost cuss, it's like they stopped a bullet just after the trigger was pulled and before it left the gun. They're amazed they stopped midword, and they're trying to see if I noticed what they almost said. And the answer is "Yes." I know what you almost said. Pastors know cuss words too. I don't say them, of course. I'm a pastor. (I'm winking at you right now.)

If they cuss in front of me, it's like they committed an unforgivable sin. The amount of red-faced apologizing that happens is pretty funny. I think they're a little surprised when I give them permission to cuss around me. Maybe that makes me a bad pastor. Feel free to be the judge of that. I'm just thankful you've read this far in the book.

If you're a parent, you know you have a funny relationship with your kid's words. Some parents lightly discipline their kids for being disrespectful, rude, and unkind in their actions but give them the maximum penalty when they say something they should not. Parents will excuse behaviors that will most certainly lead to their kid being "that" kid but feel humiliated if their kid says something they should not.

Why is your relationship with words so weird?

Your words, or lack of words, fall into four categories. The more intentional you are with your words, the better you can be at life.

SAYING THE RIGHT THING

Saying the right thing is always the best thing to say. But what is the right thing to say?

My friend Kathleen would say that's an easy question to answer. We should go with what Paul wrote: *"Do not let any unwholesome talk come out of your mouths, but only what is helpful for building others up according to their needs, that it may benefit those who listen."*

The right thing to say is always what helps build others up according to their needs. That is not how you usually define the right thing to say. You usually define it by what you "need" to say to the other person. It's about you, not them.

You think you say the right thing most of the time, but it's not up to you to decide this. It's up to the listener. You must speak up with the words that build up others.

SAYING THE WRONG THING

Have you ever just said the completely wrong thing and knew it immediately? Me neither. But I've heard of people doing this, and it's so embarrassing for them, right? Glad I cannot relate to that.

Paul wrote, *"Do not let any unwholesome talk come out of your mouths, but only what is helpful for building others up according to their needs, that it may benefit those who listen."*

So, the wrong thing to say to people are words that tear them down. Words that tear down usually come from your "need" to speak those words. Wrong words often make you feel better and benefit you. Sometimes you need to shut up.

NOT SAYING THE RIGHT THING

Not saying the right thing is not the same as saying the wrong thing. Not saying the right thing is the easiest thing to say. You avoid the right words. And you avoid the wrong words. You speak the easy words in the middle that make you feel good but don't benefit anyone.

Paul was very intentional with his words: "*Do not let any unwholesome talk come out of your mouths, but only what is helpful for building others up according to their needs, that it may benefit those who listen.*"

Not saying the right thing means you're speaking, but you're not helping. You're also not tearing down. You're just making noise. Your words are supposed to be helpful to others. You must speak up with words that help others.

NOT SAYING THE WRONG THING

We're proud of ourselves when we don't say the wrong thing. I am proud of myself a lot. I think of the wrong thing to say all the time. It's like a superpower I should not use. I even like to tell Julie, "I should get credit for not saying what I wanted to say." That's sad, I know.

But Paul wrote, *"Do not let any unwholesome talk come out of your mouths, but only what is helpful for building others up according to their needs, that it may benefit those who listen."*

Yes, what we don't say matters, but what we do say matters most. You don't get credit for not saying the wrong thing. I wish we did. You only get credit for the words you do say. So, don't just not say the wrong thing. Speak up and say the right thing.

When our oldest son Canon was in middle school, one of his guy friends called another friend, who is a girl, a rude name. It was stupid but disrespectful and mean. Of course, some other boys started calling her this name too. Ugh...middle school boys. Thankfully, Canon did not join them. He did not say the wrong thing. Good move! We were happy he made the right decision.

After a few days of this name-calling, Canon pulled his friend aside and told him to shut up. The friend didn't, of course. But, this time, Canon said the right thing, and we were proud of him.

NOW WHAT?

Life is a whole lot of talking, and it doesn't have to be spoken words. It can be written words. You are surrounded by words all day. You don't even notice most of the talking happening around you, yet it all affects you.

You can make life less complicated for you and others if you *"Do not let any unwholesome talk come out of your mouths, but only what is helpful for building others up according to their needs, that it may benefit those who listen."* Sound familiar?

So, speak up when it comes to saying the right thing.

Shut up when it comes to saying the wrong thing.

Build up others with your words.

Choose your words carefully because every word you speak matters.

Now let's turn our attention to the other simple element that makes up our complicated lives: our actions. But, just like our words, they can get complicated fast.

CONVERSATION QUESTIONS

How have you experienced the power of words positively?

How have you experienced the power of words negatively?

What comes more easily to you: saying the right thing, saying the wrong thing, not saying the right thing, or not saying the wrong thing? Why do you think this is true about you?

What steps will you take to say the right thing more often?

5

YOUR ACTIONS

Growing up and into my 20s, I hated the beach. I am hot-natured, so being on a hot, humid, sandy, crowded desert with waves of warm water was not my idea of fun or relaxing. I'm also very fair skinned. Sun poisoning is a real thing, y'all. The beach and I just did not get along.

Then one day, I started loving the beach. I think having a kid had something to do with it. I didn't want to love it. Maybe I just figured out ways to cope with my beach challenges. Sunscreen, a good book, and a t-shirt make a difference. Yes, I wear a t-shirt on the beach. Don't worry; it's a short-sleeved t-shirt. I'm not that dorky. Just average dad dorky.

So, our family started going to the beach once or twice a year. I'm biased toward east coast beaches because I love a good low tide and actual waves that make noise. We started going to Hilton Head Island, South Carolina. It's only about five hours from our house. And Julie and I started noticing something. Our entire family was different when we were there. All five of us were more relaxed. We played together more. Trust me; our trips were not perfect, but our family was different when we were there. It was good for us to be on that island. It became "our place" even though we weren't looking for a place.

So, we did what anyone else would do. We started talking about going there more often. It was fun to talk about. We'd talk about when we should go, where we should stay, where we should eat, what we'd do on the beach, etc., but talking about it was not the same as being there.

Finally, we just started going more often. Now we go multiple times every year. Many of our trips are overnighters giving us one solid day on the beach. We've even been known to drive from our house to the beach in the morning (five hours), spend the day on the beach (five hours), and drive back home that same night (five hours). Whether we're there one day or one week, it is good for our family.

Talking about something is good. But doing something is better.

LIFE IS DOING

Do you think you're aware of how significant your actions are? I don't think you are. I don't even think you're aware of most of your actions.

I did 43 actions just by typing this sentence. That is how many times one of my fingers pushed a key on my laptop just in that previous sentence. And while I thought about the sentence, I did not consciously think about pressing each key. It just kind of happened. And I think I even spelled everything correctly.

Are you aware of all your actions when you're driving? When you're driving, you're constantly looking around, you're thinking about accelerating and decelerating, you're wondering what the other driver is doing, you're singing, you're talking to the person in the car with you, you're turning on your turn signal, you're flashing your lights at that lousy driver (I'm not the only person who does that, right?), you're looking at your map app, you're turning on the AC, and so many more actions.

You easily perform millions of actions per day. I made that number up, but I feel good about it.

It's incredible, and maybe even scary, how many actions you perform without realizing it. Chalk it up to habit or instinct; humans are amazing. You do so many things without even being aware of them.

But Paul believed we should pay attention to our actions because everything we do matters. In 1 Corinthians 10:31, he wrote, *"So whether you eat or drink or whatever you do, do it all for the glory of God."*

And Colossians 3:17 he wrote, *"And whatever you do, whether in word or deed, do it all in the name of the Lord Jesus, giving thanks to God the Father through him."*

"Whatever" in both verses means "whatever." I did not look up the original language to determine that, but I feel good about my interpretation. Everything you do should be done to make God look good because you are representing Him. Is that your filter when choosing what you're going to do next?

If you take your actions seriously and believe Paul's words, every action you do should flow through this filter:

- Because I represent God, I will do this.
- When I do this, it will make God look good.

Is this your filter? Yeah, me neither. I just do a lot of things throughout each day. And sometimes, I think about what God would want me to do. But usually not.

It's funny that humans have not changed much over thousands of years. We like to think we're unique and special. We're human. We've always had an interesting relationship with our actions. In AD 57[7], Paul wrote about himself in Romans 7:15-25, *"I do not understand what I do. For what I want to do I do not do, but what I hate I do. And if I do what I do not want to do, I agree that the law is good. As it is, it is no longer I myself who do it, but it is sin living in me. For I know that good itself does not dwell in me, that is, in my sinful nature. I want to do what is good, but I cannot carry it out. For I do not do the good I want to do, but the evil I do not want to do - this I keep on doing. Now if I do what I do not want to do, it is no longer I who do it, but it is sin living in me that does it.*

So I find this law at work: Although I want to do good, evil is right there with me. For in my inner being I delight in God's law; but I see another law at work in me, waging war against the law of my mind and making me a prisoner of the law of sin at work within me. What a wretched man I am! Who will rescue me from this body that is subject to death? Thanks be to God, who delivers me through Jesus Christ our Lord!"

Before Paul was Paul, his name was Saul. When he was Saul, he literally hunted Christians to punish them. Then, one day, Jesus blinded and spoke to him about his life. That was the catalyst for Paul to start his faith in Jesus. I think being blinded and Jesus talking to me would have caused me to trust Jesus too. He became one of the most influential Christians ever to live. We're still talking about him today. And he struggled with his actions, like you and me.

Your actions confuse you. Just like Paul wrote, *"I do not understand what I do."* Ever felt that way? But when you understand your actions and get intentional about your actions, you can be better at this complicated life. Your actions can take many forms.

DOING THE RIGHT THING

I know you always do the right thing. You're you. Do you realize most people think they do the right thing most of the time? That's crazy, right? You see what they do. How could they think they're doing the right thing? Do you think anyone believes that about you? Nah. You're better than everyone else.

Most actions fall into the category of doing what you think is right. It's why you do what you do. You even think most of the "bad" things you do are the right thing to do. You know why you did it, which is what makes it right in your mind.

This has been true about people for a long, long time. The writer of Proverbs 21:2-3 warned us thousands of years ago, *"A person may think their own ways are right, but the Lord weighs the heart. To do what is right and just is more acceptable to the Lord than sacrifice."*

Gulp! You don't get to decide if your actions are the right ones. God does that. He knows your true motivation for every action you do. And He would rather you do the right thing, by His definition of "right," than make sacrifices to Him.

Maybe all your actions that are right in your mind are not always the right things to do. How can you know that what you're doing is the right thing to do? We'll talk about that in a few pages.

DOING THE WRONG THING

I'm a pastor. I get a front-row seat to people doing the wrong thing. It's a perk of the job. Watching people mess up their complicated lives is a ton of motivation not to do what I see other people do.

You can relate to Paul. *"For I have the desire to do what is good, but I cannot carry it out. For I do not do the good I want to do, but the evil I do not want to do - this I keep on doing."*

It's interesting. You rarely do the wrong thing believing it is the wrong thing to do. You typically do something thinking it is the right thing to do or just something neutral to do and are surprised when it turns out to be the wrong thing.

There's another thing about doing the wrong thing. Let's be painfully honest here. There are times you intentionally do the wrong thing. Why? It makes you feel good. The other person deserves it. Ever justified a wrong action with one of those reasons? Paul was just like us: *"What a wretched man I am! Who will rescue me from this body that is subject to death?"* We complicate life for ourselves and others."

NOT DOING THE RIGHT THING

Not doing the right thing is not the same as doing the wrong thing. Not doing the right thing is easy. You don't do the wrong thing, but you don't do the right thing. You just do something. It's the lazy thing to do, but at least it's doing something.

"Someone else will do it." I've thought that plenty of times in my life. It is my way of excusing my lack of right actions. I make it someone else's responsibility to do the right thing. How sad. Aren't you glad you're not me?

James, the brother of Jesus, wrote in James 4:17, *"If anyone, then, knows the good they ought to do and doesn't do it, it is sin for them."* So, it's a sin when we don't do the right thing. Ouch! That hurts. Doing the wrong thing is a sin. That's obvious. But not doing the right thing is sin? Deep down, we know it's true.

Remember, Paul wrote, *"For in my inner being I delight in God's law; but I see another law at work in me, waging war against the law of my mind and making me a prisoner of the law of sin at work within me."* You have the same internal tension in you that Paul described so well. It's more than an angel on one shoulder and the devil on your other shoulder. That's a cute picture of a real battle taking place in you. You want to do the right thing God wants you to do. That "force" is strong in you. But there is another "force" in you - sin. And sin is powerful, too.

NOT DOING THE WRONG THING

Not doing the wrong thing does not mean you did the right thing. It just means you avoided the wrong actions. And you get some credit for this. Not doing the wrong thing is a good thing. Imagine a world where the minimum people did was not do the wrong action. What a better world this would be.

When it comes to our actions, this should be the starting line. As you take your actions seriously, start with not doing the wrong things. Others won't notice what you don't do. But you'll know you're being intentional with your actions. The more wrong things you don't do, the more motivated you will be to do the right thing.

Is this going to be easy? No. Paul's words are sobering, *"For what I want to do I do not do, but what I hate I do."* And, *"For I know that good itself does not dwell in me, that is, in my sinful nature."*

Not doing the wrong thing seems like the least we could do. And, in a way, it is. Sometimes, though, the easiest things to do are the most difficult.

THE RIGHT THING TO DO - ALWAYS

Whew! After all that, is it even possible for you to do the right thing? Yes!

Paul, the same guy who wrote Romans 7:15-25, also wrote Galatians 6:9-10, *"Let us not become weary in doing good, for at the proper time we will reap a harvest if we do not give up. Therefore, as we have opportunity, let us do good to all people, especially to those who belong to the family of believers."*

I love Paul's honesty. Doing the right thing will take effort. It is possible you will grow tired, impatient, and worn out while you're trying to do the right thing. Don't let those temporary emotions and feelings win. You will see the benefits of doing the right thing. It may take time, but you'll know why it was the right thing.

A big question: Can you honestly know the right thing to do in every situation? Yes. But doesn't God determine if what you're doing is the right thing? Yes. Clarity is kind, and God is kind. He makes it clear what the right thing is to do.

In Matthew 22:34-40, Matthew wrote down this conversation between Jesus and some religious leaders, *"Hearing that Jesus had silenced the Sadducees, the*

Pharisees got together. One of them, an expert in the law, tested him with this question: 'Teacher, which is the greatest commandment in the Law?'

Jesus replied: 'Love the Lord your God with all your heart and with all your soul and with all your mind.' This is the first and greatest commandment. And the second is like it: 'Love your neighbor as yourself.' All the Law and the Prophets hang on these two commandments.'"

This wasn't a friendly conversation. The religious leaders were trying to trick Jesus into slipping up so they could condemn and punish him, and his answer to their question shut them up. They knew he was right.

In 1 John 4:7-12, John gave us even more clarity on what is always the right thing to do. *"Dear friends, let us love one another, for love comes from God. Everyone who loves has been born of God and knows God. Whoever does not love does not know God, because God is love. This is how God showed his love among us: He sent his one and only Son into the world that we might live through him. This is love: not that we loved God, but that he loved us and sent his Son as an atoning sacrifice for our sins. Dear friends, since God so loved us, we also ought to love one another. No one has ever seen God; but if we love one another, God lives in us and his love is made complete in us."*

Life is complicated. And you often make knowing the right thing to do complicated. But it's not. The right thing to do is not easy. But it's not complicated.

How can you always get your actions right? What is always the right thing to do?

Love.

If you've been hurt by love, stick with me.

If love feels too touchy-feely, stick with me.

If love sounds too simple, stick with me.

WHAT IS LOVE?

I love Julie. I literally cannot express to you how much I love her. And she cannot understand how much I love her. I do my best to show her I love her. I bring her flowers. I run errands for her. I sit on the couch with her. We go on dates. I don't say everything I am thinking. I get her gas. I don't give her gas. Sorry, that was too easy. I am not perfect, but I do many things to show her how much I love her.

I learned many years ago that what I did to show Julie love only mattered if she felt loved. My motivation, intent, and actions only count if she feels loved by me. If she does not feel loved, I need to change my actions to show her love. Of course! I don't show her love so I feel good about myself. I show her love so she feels loved by me. It took me too long to learn this. Sorry, Julie.

In John 15:12-13, Jesus said, *"My command is this: Love each other as I have loved you. Greater love has no one than this: to lay down one's life for one's friends."* Jesus loves you so much he died for you. He stretched our definition of love to the point that we'd need to die for the other person to show true love. Loving someone is not for or about you. Loving someone is about them. If the other person does not feel loved, it is not love.

John wrote in 1 John 4:10, *"This is love: not that we loved God, but that he loved us and sent his Son as an atoning sacrifice for our sins."* Love is God sending his Son to die for your sins. His love for you is about you.

Love is doing what is best for the other person.

Love is making the other person feel loved.

46

Love is always the right thing to do.

HOW TO LOVE EVERYONE

How do you show others love when life is so complicated? That can get, well, complicated. We all feel loved in unique ways. I feel loved by my coworkers differently than I feel loved by my family. I used to feel loved by Julie when she spoke encouraging words to me. Now I feel loved when she touches me. Loving others can get complicated.

Loving everyone can also get complicated because it's easier to love people like yourself. If they voted for someone different...if they cheer for another team...if they believe in something you don't...if they support something you don't...you get the point. Loving everyone is complicated.

Once again, God is kind. He clarifies how to show love to all people: family, friends, coworkers, strangers, enemies, etc.

In 1 Corinthians 13:4-7, Paul wrote what love looks like. Unfortunately, we only look at what he wrote through the lens of romantic love. These are the go-to verses for pastors to read at weddings. It's a shame. Paul did not have romantic love or weddings in mind when he wrote these words. He had ordinary people living complicated lives in mind. This is the kind of love we should show everyone every day, no matter who they are, what they believe, how they act, or how much they complicate our lives.

"Love is patient, love is kind. It does not envy, it does not boast, it is not proud. It does not dishonor others, it is not self-seeking, it is not easily angered, it keeps no record of wrongs. Love does not delight in evil but rejoices with the truth. It always protects, always trusts, always hopes, always perseveres."

Is loving people this way easy? No. Is it complicated? Yes. Is it clear? Yes.

It's so clear I'm not going to elaborate on it. The right thing to do all the time is to love everyone as Paul described. Period.

The right thing to do at all times is to love the person in front of you. In John 14:23–24, John wrote these words, *"Jesus replied, 'Anyone who loves me will obey my teaching. My Father will love them, and we will come to them and make our home with them. Anyone who does not love me will not obey my teaching. These words you hear are not my own; they belong to the Father who sent me.'"*

If you love Jesus, you will do what he wants you to do. And he wants you to love other people. Matthew, Mark, Luke, and John give you examples of how he loved other people. And, by the way, Jesus lived a really complicated life.

John wrote in 1 John 4:7–12, *"Dear friends, let us love one another, for love comes from God. Everyone who loves has been born of God and knows God. Whoever does not love does not know God, because God is love. This is how God showed his love among us: He sent his one and only Son into the world that we might live through him. This is love: not that we loved God, but that he loved us and sent his Son as an atoning sacrifice for our sins. Dear friends, since God so loved us, we also ought to love one another. No one has ever seen God; but if we love one another, God lives in us and his love is made complete in us."*

God loved you and showed you His love for you by allowing His Son to die for you. You love other people because God loved you first. If you don't show love to everyone, you do not know God. Wow! That's clarity. If you love the people around you, the Holy Spirit lives in you, and you experience His love for you.

A lot is riding on you doing the right thing.

But...

Life is complicated. Showing love is complicated. When things get complicated, you feel afraid. You may not want to admit you're scared, but fear creeps in. John continues in 1 John 4:18-21, *"There is no fear in love. But perfect love drives out fear, because fear has to do with punishment. The one who fears is not made perfect in love.*

We love because he first loved us. Whoever claims to love God yet hates a brother or sister is a liar. For whoever does not love their brother and sister, whom they have seen, cannot love God, whom they have not seen. And he has given us this command: Anyone who loves God must also love their brother and sister."

The more you do the right thing. The more you show love. The less fear you will feel even when the situation or the person is complicated. Less fear does not mean it will be less complicated, but it will be easier to do the right thing.

NOW WHAT?

You show love through your words and actions. Sound familiar?

Speak words that cause whoever is near you to feel loved by you. If the person does not feel loved, find new words to say.

Act in ways that cause the person in front of you to feel loved. Paul gives you a list of ways to show love to people. People like me need it spelled out for them. The receiver of your love must feel loved.

Love is always the right thing to say and do.

You can make life less complicated for yourself and others if you pay attention to your actions and do the right thing. You can be more intentional about your actions. And you really can show all people love. It's not about you. It's about them. And it starts with the love you receive from your Heavenly Father.

Now that we know the two most basic ingredients of life are words and actions, we can be better at living this complicated life. It just takes a step.

CONVERSATION QUESTIONS

How do you decide if what you're doing is the right thing to do?

When have you done the wrong thing but initially thought it was the right thing?

What was your gut reaction to this: "Life is complicated. And we often make knowing the right thing to do complicated. But it's not. The right thing to do is not easy, but it's not complicated."

Whom do you find difficult to love? What steps will you take to make them feel loved by you?

6

LIFE IS STEPS

J ulie is directionally challenged. Are you aware of this disorder? She
has so many strengths, but getting from one place to another place
is not one of them. We've tried old-school folded maps, hand-drawn
maps, verbal directions, text-only directions, every map app available using
verbal directions, every map app available using visual directions, directions
using landmarks, directions using street names, and directions using cardinal
directions. She has difficulty getting somewhere whether it is five minutes or
five hours from our house. We've lived where we currently live for 14 years,
and she does not know how to get to most places. Thankfully, we all just
laugh when it happens.

On one of our trips to Hilton Head, our sons and I were in Washington, DC
on the day we were supposed to check in. So, Julie drove by herself and we
flew. I texted Julie the address of the gas station where she should stop on
the way. She put the address into her map app and hit the road. She followed
the step-by-step directions, but she did not end up at the correct address.
She did not even end up in the correct city. Thankfully, Dudley, Georgia is not
far from Dublin, Georgia. To this day, we do not know how this happened, or
how this keeps happening.

Getting from where you are to where you want to go always requires a series of steps. That is true driving from one place to another. That is true in losing weight. And that is true in life.

Life is a series of steps. You want it to be like taking steps along a straight, smoothly paved sidewalk. You walk along the sidewalk at the pace you choose. You can see far ahead, and your steps take you exactly where you want to go. You never stumble or fall. Wouldn't that be nice?

Instead, life is like taking steps through the woods with no trail to follow. Even if you know where you want to end up, your path to get there is anything but straight. The uneven ground causes you to veer off the straight line you think you're walking. The change in elevation causes you to slow down and then speed up. Then there are the trees, rocks, and debris you must walk around. Those same things cause you not to be able to see too far ahead because you must keep your eyes on the ground. You can only see just far enough ahead for your next step or two. You may not fall, but you're bound to stumble on a loose rock or stick. Ultimately, you do end up somewhere.

After finding out about my infertility issues, our steps were very different from the steps we thought we'd be taking. These steps involved multiple doctor's visits and procedures, almost adopting a child, spending lots of money, and receiving support from special friends and family.

While we were taking these unexpected steps, we were also taking steps in our jobs, marriage, friendships, hobbies, etc. The rest of our lives did not slow down to acknowledge this new situation.

Remember the definition of "complicated?"

1: consisting of parts intricately combined
2: difficult to analyze, understand, or explain[8]

That was the definition of our life then - and today. Even on the good days, this is our life. Can you relate?

How do we deal with a complicated life? Steps. One step at a time.

STEPS

What is a step? It is a decision to say something or do something. You take a bunch of steps each day. "A bunch" is the closest I could get to being numerically accurate.

Steps scare you. Even good steps. When we got married, those steps were scary. Our infertility steps were scary. The new steps we took when each kid was born were scary. When Julie began to teach at a new school, those steps were scary. When our daughter started college, those steps were scary. When my dad was diagnosed with dementia, those steps were scary. When I started writing this book, those steps were scary.

Steps are scary because you can never know precisely where that step will take you. I try hard to predict and control where my steps will lead me. I can be intentional and wise with my steps, but I cannot control what happens after I take that step. Maybe you've heard me mention this: life is complicated.

But, and this is a big but, you can confidently take steps. Not confident in yourself, but confident in God. In Romans 8:22-28, Paul wrote, *"We know that the whole creation has been groaning as in the pains of childbirth right up to the present time. Not only so, but we ourselves, who have the first fruits of the Spirit, groan inwardly as we wait eagerly for our adoption to sonship, the redemption of our bodies. For in this hope we were saved. But hope that is seen is no hope at all. Who hopes for what they already have? But if we hope for what we do not yet have, we wait for it patiently.*

In the same way, the Spirit helps us in our weakness. We do not know what we ought to pray for, but the Spirit himself intercedes for us through wordless groans. And he who searches our hearts knows the mind of the Spirit, because the Spirit intercedes for God's people in accordance with the will of God.

And we know that in all things God works for the good of those who love him, who have been called according to his purpose."

I love the honesty of the Bible. Paul's use of the word "groan" describes how you feel about living a complicated life. You often don't have the words to express how you feel. But you mentally, emotionally, and spiritually groan because life is complicated. It's like you subconsciously know there is something better out there. You're just waiting and hoping for it. Until then, you groan.

And here comes God! His Spirit, Who lives inside of you if you have started your faith in Jesus, helps you. His Spirit even prays for you because He knows what you need more than you know what you need. Thank You, God!

Here is the difficult-to-understand but amazing truth: *"in all things God works for the good of those who love him."*

If you have faith in Jesus, God works for your good in all things. As you speak and act. As you take steps. God is working for your good. What exactly does that mean? I don't know. But I know it is good. I know God is working for my good. And I know God works for your good if you put your faith in His Son.

I can take scary steps with confidence because of this truth.

I can look back on the two years in a row I was an idiot in college and broke up with Julie on her birthday and say, "God worked that out for good."

I can look back decades after finding out about our infertility issues and say, "God worked that out for good."

I can look back on my dad's dementia and say, "God worked that out for good."

I can look back on the good and bad parts of my life and say, "God worked that out for good." Does that mean everything worked out as I wanted it to or even better than I expected? Nope. But I can see how God worked for good. And where I cannot, I trust Him.

Søren Kierkegaard was a Danish theologian, philosopher, and writer. I'm not a Kierkegaard expert; I had to copy and paste his name here because his name is so different, but I know he was brilliant. In one of his journals, he wrote,

"It is quite true what philosophy says, that life must be understood backwards. But then one forgets the other principle, that it must be lived forward. Which principle, the more one thinks it through, ends exactly with temporal life never being able to be properly understood, precisely because I can at no instant find complete rest to adopt the position: backward."[9]

Excuse me? Thankfully, other people did not understand what he wrote either. Glad it was not just me. People a long time ago condensed his journal entry to this statement so we could all understand what he meant:

"Life can only be understood backwards; but it must be lived forwards."

Living forwards requires steps. As we step, we can trust God is working for our good. Let's dive deeper into our steps and how we move through this complicated life.

STANDING STILL IS NOT SAFE

We live outside of Atlanta, Georgia. We love where we live. Atlanta is known for many things: music, movies, arts, culture, traffic, and sports. (If you bring up the Falcons' loss to the Patriots in Super Bowl 51, I disrespectfully ask you to stop reading this book.)

The traffic in and around Atlanta is nasty. That's the most accurate word I can use to describe it. Traffic is always bad around here; fortunately, you never know just how bad it's going to be.

Years ago, the traffic helped me identify a personal core value. We've all got specific things we value over all other things. One of my core values is progress. Movement. This shows up in my work, relationships, self-leadership, and, yes, in traffic.

Standing still in traffic takes me to a dark place. Just ask my family. On second thought, it's better if you don't ask them about this. What happens in the car should stay in the car.

You think you want to move forward and achieve your goals, accumulate more money or things, experience better relationships, etc. You know you're supposed to want to make progress. But...

If you pray, have you paid attention to what you pray for? Have you listened to other people's prayers or prayer requests?

It seems like the thing you want most from God is for Him to help you stand still and not move forward. You pray for peace, calm, clarity, ease, safety, etc. The opposite of steps. You value shallow water. In shallow water, you can put both feet on the ground and not have to move.

While you know you need to take steps, you desire to stand still. Standing still feels safe and easy, but it is dangerous. It gives you a false sense of rest.

Standing is not stepping. Standing allows the complications of life to gather and build up around you. It complicates life more. Standing still actually makes taking the next step more difficult.

Let's get scientific for a moment. PhysicsClassroom.com says,

"Newton's first law of motion states that 'An object at rest stays at rest and an object in motion stays in motion with the same speed and in the same direction unless acted upon by an unbalanced force.' Objects tend to 'keep on doing what they're doing.' In fact, it is the natural tendency of objects to resist changes in their state of motion. This tendency to resist changes in their state of motion is described as inertia.

Inertia: the resistance an object has to a change in its state of motion.

Galileo, a premier scientist in the seventeenth century, developed the concept of inertia. Galileo reasoned that moving objects eventually stop because of a force called friction."[10]

You are meant to be in motion taking steps, living in this complicated life, God working for your good. Before Galileo discovered inertia, people believed objects in motion just came to a stop. Galileo discovered things in motion come to a stop only because of friction.

What stops you from taking steps? Your friction is your complicated life. It entices you to stop moving, and you believe the lie that standing still is the goal. You believe standing still is the safest posture to take when, in fact, it is dangerous to stand still.

There are two kinds of steps you can take through life. One complicates life even more. The other helps you be better at this complicated life.

BACKWARD STEPS

Have you ever made a wrong decision? Yeah, me neither. But, boy, do I know some people who have!

I'm kidding, of course. I have made some bad decisions in my life. Dumb decisions. Stupid decisions. What-was-I-thinking decisions.

You make mistakes. Those are the "oops" moments in your life. Those are when you accidentally do something that is not a big deal. Oops, you were speeding. Oops, you overate. Oops, you overbooked your schedule. Oops, you missed class. Oops, you took a wrong turn.

Bad decisions are not mistakes. Bad decisions are intentional choices you make that are the wrong thing to do. Everyone does this. God calls it sin.

Paul wrote in Romans 3:23, "*...for all have sinned and fall short of the glory of God.*"

John wrote in 1 John 1:8, 10, "*If we claim to be without sin, we deceive ourselves and the truth is not in us. If we claim we have not sinned, we make him out to be a liar and his word is not in us.*"

The prophet Isaiah wrote in Isaiah 64:6, "*All of us have become like one who is unclean, and all our righteous acts are like filthy rags; we all shrivel up like a leaf, and like the wind our sins sweep us away.*" Geez. Isaiah had quite a way with words.

You sin. I sin. They sin. Just because everyone sins does not make it okay. And it does not mean someone does not have the right to call out your sin.

Since life is made up of steps, let's call sin taking a step backward. Any time you decide to do the wrong thing, you're taking a step backward. Everyone sins.

You experience so many people doing the wrong thing and taking steps backward, you become numb to it. You think, "No big deal." Sin is always a big deal. When you take a step backward, you complicate your life even more. You complicate others' lives.

You are going to take steps backward. No one can be perfect, but you must do something about your sin. I believe you can take fewer steps backward. How can you sin less and take fewer steps backward?

Paul is here to help you with this question. In 1 Corinthians 16:13-14, he wrote, *"Be on your guard; stand firm in the faith; be courageous; be strong. Do everything in love."*

AVOID YOUR SIN TRIGGERS

One way to take fewer steps backward is to recognize what causes you to take these steps. If you can identify the times and situations that make it more likely for you to sin, you can avoid them. Paul called this, *"be on your guard."* Be on the lookout. Defend yourself against the things that cause you to sin. Your sin always, not sometimes, complicates your life and the lives of those around you.

When are you more likely to sin and take a step backward? Maybe when you are:

· tired

- hungry
- tempted
- ignoring reality
- drinking alcohol
- prideful
- minimizing the effects of your sin
- selfish
- using drugs
- selfish
- insecure
- around someone who is a bad influence
- _____ (insert your greatest sin trigger)

Determine your sin triggers. Be on your guard. Avoid your sin triggers. Sin less. Take fewer steps backward.

I know it's not as easy as I make it sound. Sin is powerful. The things that lead you to sin are powerful. But, and this is a big but, Paul wrote in Romans 6:1-2, 6, "*What shall we say, then? Shall we go on sinning so that grace may increase? By no means! We are those who have died to sin; how can we live in it any longer?*

For we know that our old self was crucified with him so that the body ruled by sin might be done away with, that we should no longer be slaves to sin - because anyone who has died has been set free from sin."

You are a new person if you have started your faith in Jesus. (More on that in the next chapter.) The old you was a slave to sin. You've felt that before, right? We all have. But when you put your trust in Jesus, you were set free from sin. That does not mean you don't sin anymore or are not tempted to sin. It just means you are no longer controlled by sin. God's Spirit in you now controls you. He is in you. You can be on your guard and avoid sin.

LOVE MORE

Paul gives you a familiar way to sin less and take fewer steps backward. He wrote, *"Do everything in love."* Do the right thing! What is always the right thing to do? Love. How do you guard yourself against sin? How do you take fewer steps backward? Love other people in a way they feel loved by you.

Backward steps are selfish. You take these steps to protect yourself or get what you want. In the end, you lose.

Forward steps are for other people. You take these steps to do what is best for them and to make them feel loved. In the end, you win.

When you show love to others in ways that make them feel loved, you take fewer steps backward. It is difficult to sin when you actively love those around you.

STEPS FORWARD

Another way to avoid taking steps backward is to take steps forward. The more forward steps you take, the fewer backward steps you take. The best way to live in a complicated world is to take forward steps consistently. Let's talk more about this.

FORWARD STEPS

Did you get your steps in today?

I like to protect the identity of my weird friends. I won't share their names to protect their successful names and careers. Besides, they know way too much about me. They could go on tour sharing weird stories about me.

One group of weirdos used to have a steps contest on Sundays. I worked at a large church with a large building. We walked a lot on Sundays. These friends would compare step counts throughout the morning and declare a winner at the end of Sunday. They'd pass 10,000 steps before lunch usually.

My favorite weird friends are those who wear devices on their wrists that count their steps. In meetings, they just start swinging their arms while they are sitting in a chair. These weirdos are getting their devices to give them credit for steps even though they are sitting down. I respect them just for the creativity of their cheating. Whatever it takes to get credit for 10,000 steps.

Did you know the idea of 10,000 steps being the number of steps you should take in a day to keep you healthy did not come from a doctor or anyone in the medical field? "The origins of the number go back to 1965 when a Japanese company made a device named *Manpo-kei*, which translates to '10,000 steps meter.'"[11] The company's pedometer was named 10,000 steps because they thought the name would help them sell more products. They thought the name would catch on. I don't know if the name caught on, but the number sure did.

Ten thousand steps have become fixed in our thinking and actions. In 2019, Dr. I-Min Lee, a physician and professor of medicine at Harvard Medical School, looked into the validity of 10,000 steps being our benchmark. She and her team learned, "Mortality rates progressively improved before leveling off at approximately 7,500 steps per day."[12] So what?

You benefit greatly from taking 7,500 steps per day. You don't benefit that much from taking over 7,500 steps per day. If you're one of those 10,000-step people, you can take an extended vacation from walking. Those extra 2,500 steps per day you've been taking have earned you some time off from walking. So, sit down. Prop your feet up. Binge-watch a show. Watch other people walk around, and just smile as they try to reach their incorrect goal of 10,000 steps.

The only way to live well in this complicated life is to take steps forward.
Want life to feel less complicated? Want more money? Want stronger
relationships? Want a different job? Want better faith? Take steps in a
forward direction.

My friends Ben and Jackie took a forward step when they realized their autistic
daughter was a few years away from aging out of school. They knew there
would not be many opportunities for Jordyn. So, they stopped standing still.
Standing still was easy. But it kept them focused on what was not available
to her. They took a forward step to create an opportunity. What was their
forward step? It was pretty simple, but it changed their lives.

Their forward step was creating a t-shirt that read, "Be Kind To Everyone."
Their goals were to sell 40 shirts and, in doing so, teach Jordyn some job skills.
That was years ago. Check out BeKindToEveryone.com to see how it's going
today. And maybe buy a shirt. I've got a few.

Here are some things to keep in mind as you take forward steps through life.

STEPS ARE NOT SEXY

Steps are not very exciting. "Exciting" is another word for "sexy." Julie
said I should explain myself quickly. Jumping is exciting. Dancing is exciting,
unless you're like me and don't have rhythm. Running is exciting. Sprinting
is even more exciting. But life is best lived by taking steps. Consistent
steps forward lead you to live well in a complicated life. Steps can seem
so insignificant, yet every step is meaningful.

You seek sexy. You think consistent and steady are boring. You believe life
happens in big, significant steps. You think people should notice our steps.
Please don't believe what is not true.

STEP TOWARD PEOPLE

Your biggest regrets in life will involve people. Your most significant wins in life will include people. Other people always matter most. Take steps toward better relationships with people. Start, repair, or grow your connections with people. Just being kind to a stranger is a step forward.

I was literally in stand-still traffic in downtown Atlanta when I got the call that my friend Jake had a heart attack. Have I mentioned how much I hate not moving when I am driving? Sitting in traffic at the 14th Street exit, I knew it wasn't good, and he may not live. For days, Julie and I talked with his wife, Kristi, about what the doctors were saying. To make a very long story short, he lived. I was so mad at him for scaring me like that. I may have told him that in a text while he was still in the hospital. I'm a good friend in that way.

His heart attack made me realize my friendship with him was one of the biggest wins in my life. I've taken many steps toward Jake over the many years we've known each other, and he has taken many steps toward me. Our steps toward each other are what have made our relationship so meaningful today.

My friend Richard also had a heart attack. He died. I was in shock when I heard the news. We were talking about doing some projects together. We had only known each other for a short time, but I regret not taking more steps toward him. Our relationship was built mainly on the steps he took toward me.

Take steps toward every person in front of you throughout the day. Make sure they feel loved by you. Life is more about people than tasks and accomplishments.

What are some possible steps toward people you can take today?

• forgive someone

- accept someone
- care for someone
- encourage someone
- carry someone's worry with them
- put up with someone difficult
- be kind to someone
- honor someone
- live in harmony with someone
- serve someone
- greet someone

You can take these steps toward family, friends, and strangers. All people need you to take steps toward them.

A Personal Public Service Announcement: Sometimes, the best step forward with someone can be a step away from them. If someone is toxic or dangerous to you, take a forward step away from them. Julie and I have not had to do this too often. We're fortunate. We did have a friend from our past we had to take a forward step away from. We stood still in this friendship for too long. The longer we stood still, the more complicated life got. When we finally took a forward step away from him, it made life much less complicated.

THE NORMAL STEPS MATTER MORE THAN THE BIG STEPS

I used to think the steps I needed to take in life were only the "big" steps. You know the ones I'm talking about. Do I quit my job to start a new career? Do we move? Do I get serious about my relationship with that person? What should my college major be?

You often think about forward steps as these types of big decisions. They can be, but there's a funny thing about steps. The more "normal" forward steps you take each day, the better you get at taking the big steps. Does that mean the big steps get easy? No. You get better at taking those big steps and knowing the forward step to take in this big decision.

Take the normal steps. The everyday, ordinary, seemingly insignificant forward steps you take matter. They may matter the most.

THE NEXT STEP

You are conditioned to take a forward step and then take a break. Step. Stand still. Step. Stand still. From time to time, you take a forward step and are tempted to take a backward step. "One step forward, two steps back." Sound familiar? Step. Backward step. Step. Step. Backward step. You don't see yourself as capable of consistent and continuous stepping. Step. Step. Step. Step.

When you see your day as opportunity after opportunity to take steps forward, you will look for your next forward step. The next step becomes the most critical step. Life may or may not get less complicated, but you can live better in this complicated life.

Remember, a step is a decision to say something or do something. A forward step is a decision to say or do the right thing. You can decide to say and do the right thing throughout each day. The more right things you say and do each day, the more forward steps you take, and the better you get at taking the next step forward. Step. Step. Step. Step.

What happens when we learn to do this? The writer of Psalms wrote in 37:23-24, *"The Lord makes firm the steps of the one who delights in him; though he may stumble, he will not fall, for the Lord upholds him with his hand."* "Though he may stumble...." Life is complicated. You will lose your balance. You will trip. "...he will not fall." You can keep taking forward steps. You will not fall.

NOW WHAT?

Jesus started a movement that has lasted for thousands of years and has grown worldwide. If you can do that, you have my attention. What did Jesus do? He took forward steps. The writer of Hebrews wrote in Hebrews 12:1-3, *"Therefore, since we are surrounded by such a great cloud of witnesses, let us throw off everything that hinders and the sin that so easily entangles. And let us run with perseverance the race marked out for us, fixing our eyes on Jesus, the pioneer and perfecter of faith. For the joy set before him he endured the cross, scorning its shame, and sat down at the right hand of the throne of God. Consider him who endured such opposition from sinners, so that you will not grow weary and lose heart."*

We only have access to three years of Jesus' life. We can observe his life in the books called Matthew, Mark, Luke, John, and Acts in the Bible. Over and over and over, Jesus took forward steps *"for the joy set before him."* You and I and everyone else were the joy set before him. He took forward steps toward you to make you feel loved.

What is your next step? I don't know. Don't think big step. Think normal step. What is the next right thing for you to say or do? Look for it. Do it. Take a step forward. Now say or do the next right thing. Step forward. Now the next right thing. Step forward. You got this!

It may feel like it, but you are not walking through this complicated life with a blindfold. Your eyes can see, but they can only see a short distance ahead. Dr. Martin Luther King, Jr. once said, "Faith is taking the first step even when you don't see the whole staircase."[13] Take the next right forward step even when you do not know what comes next.

I'm writing this as much for me as I am for you. I naturally think strategically. That means I naturally think far ahead and see how things connect. It's a good thing sometimes. It's a bad thing other times. That, along with my love of control, means I think I can control what will happen in the future. So, I plan out too many steps ahead. Life is too complicated for that. I've learned, and am still learning, to take one forward step at a time. Then take the next step. Then the next.

What is your next step? Don't step backward. Don't stand still. Don't get fooled into thinking you have to jump or sprint ahead. What is the next forward step you should take?

CONVERSATION QUESTIONS

When have you experienced God working for your good?

When do you typically pray for peace, calm, clarity, ease, safety, etc.? Have you ever considered standing still may not be good for you?

What is your biggest current sin? I'm kidding! You don't have to answer that.

What are some of your sin triggers?

What forward steps should you take right now?

7

FAITH

For most of his life, my dad believed faith was not something you should discuss. It was too personal and would only cause problems if you brought it up. Later in his life, he regretted that decision. It caused problems not bringing it up. Faith is the most important thing about a person. Unfortunately, when you make a topic off-limits, you make it feel more complicated than it is.

You have faith. What kind of faith do you have? Does it feel temporary and fragile? Or is it eternal and unbreakable? That seems like a crucial distinction when it comes to our faith.

In the rest of the book chapters, we will look at faith. Specifically, how to experience your faith, so it does not feel disappointing. Yes, it's okay to admit your faith feels disappointing, but it's not okay to assume it just has to be that way.

Something in you says faith should be powerful and meaningful. Yet, your experience with it is usually weak and confusing. You feel like "This is it?" when you should feel like "This is it!"

I want you to have faith that causes you to feel like, "This is it!" It's not perfect faith. It's not a one-size-fits-all faith. It's *your* faith. It's a fulfilling faith, no matter what happens. And a lot is going to happen. I think faith can be more than what you've grown to accept.

8

WHAT IS FAITH?

My friend John Woodall once said, "You rise and fall on the definition of your words." He's right.

How do you define "love?" It's such a common word. But what does it mean? Does it mean the same thing each time you say the word? Of course not. Let's pick on me for a minute. I love:

- Julie
- Chick-fil-A
- Diet Dr. Pepper
- my kids
- driving
- thunderstorms
- Atlanta sports
- adidas
- Hilton Head Island
- watching my kids play sports
- results
- Jesus

I love every one of these things, but my love for Julie and my love for Chick-fil-A are different. Friends who know me well may say there is not much difference, but there is. I promise.

I have told Julie, "I love you."

I have told Julie, "I love Chick-fil-A." Don't judge me.

She believes me when I say both statements. Thank God she understands I don't define the word "love" the same way in both statements. If she believed I feel the same way about her that I feel about a restaurant that sells chicken, there would be problems.

"Love" cannot mean the same thing for each one of the things on my list. If it did, I'm a sad human. Let's not debate that right now.

Think about the word "soon." How do you define it? Does "soon" mean in the next 10 minutes? In the next hour or two? By tomorrow? This week? It can mean all those things.

When Julie asks me to change the batteries in our smoke detectors, I usually answer, "I will soon." What do I mean? I'll get to it in the next week or so. It will get done.

When I ask Julie, "Are we having dinner soon?" I mean in the next five minutes. Hanger is a real thing, y'all.

Same word. Coming out of my mouth both times. And I mean two different things. Definitions are important.

"Faith" is another one of those common words you say a lot, but you mean so many different things when you say it.

WHAT FAITH IS NOT

As you know, our family loves the beach on Hilton Head Island, and we love taking walks on the beach. Teague, our youngest, loves to find shark teeth as we walk along the shoreline. I love helping him find them...for about three minutes. For every shark tooth I find, I see 10,000 things that look like shark teeth but are not shark teeth. 10,000 might be a bit of an exaggeration, but it sure feels like that many to me.

Teague has taught me numerous times how to identify the real thing, but I think anything black, white, or gray that is triangular has to be a shark tooth. And I'm usually wrong. They're fakes.

Fake faith is all around you.

"Faith" is such a positive word. You feel good about yourself and just feel good in general whenever you use the word. But when you believe faith is something it is not, it is guaranteed to disappoint you. Let's look at some things faith is not.

POSITIVE THINKING

Faith is not wishful thinking. "Faith" sounds like the perfect word for an inspirational quote, but faith is usually the opposite of easy. It can be and usually is difficult. When you make it sound sweet and soft, you admit you don't know what faith is.

BELIEVING STRONG ENOUGH

If you just believe in yourself. If you just believe strong enough. If you just try hard enough. Faith is not "If you just...." Faith does not depend on your effort. Faith is the opposite of your effort. Faith has almost nothing to do with how hard you want or work for something.

CORRECT BELIEFS

While believing correctly can make your faith more meaningful, correct beliefs do not result in faith. You can even believe all the right things and have no faith. James, the brother of Jesus, wrote in James 2:19: *"You believe that there is one God. Good! Even the demons believe that – and shudder."*

BLIND BELIEF

If you believe trust is like putting a blindfold over your eyes and walking through life, I have good news. That is not faith. Faith is not blind trust. If trust is blind, it is not faith. Faith puts its trust in something or someone.

PERFECTION

Nowhere, I repeat, nowhere is there any expectation that faith means perfection. In Matthew 14:29-31, we read about the time Peter walked on water. *"'Come,' he said. Then Peter got down out of the boat, walked on the water and came toward Jesus. But when he saw the wind, he was afraid and, beginning to sink, cried out, 'Lord, save me!'*

Immediately Jesus reached out his hand and caught him. 'You of little faith,' he said, 'why did you doubt?'"

This is the same Peter who would later deny Jesus three times. This is the same Peter whom Jesus tells in Matthew 16:18, *"And I tell you that you are Peter, and on this rock I will build my church, and the gates of Hades will not overcome it."*

Peter had anything but perfect faith. His faith was messy. And Jesus established the church through him. Genuine faith is not perfect faith.

CERTAINTY

Author and speaker Anne Lamott wrote, "The opposite of faith is not doubt, but certainty."[14] If faith is certainty, it would not be faith. It would be knowledge. Even though faith is not certainty, you can have confidence in the midst of trust.

CHURCHY ACTIVITIES

It feels like we must perform and act right to earn anything in most areas of our lives. If that's true, it must be true about our faith. We often think we have strong faith when we're busy doing churchy things.

Peter Scazzero is a pastor, mentor, and author. He wrote, "When the people ask about the 'works' God requires, they have in mind things such as prayer, acts of mercy, giving, or Bible study. Surprisingly, Jesus says there is only one work – 'To believe in the one [God] has sent.' This phrase believe in [him] means to trust in him – and not just once but continually – in an ongoing, moment-by-moment, and day-by-day kind of way."[15]

MORALISTIC THERAPEUTIC DEISM

This may come as a surprise, but I did not come up with those words. Christian Smith and Melinda Lundquist Denton get the credit for this term. Moralistic Therapeutic Deism is the term they use to describe how people define their faith. Here is what they observed:

- Moralism equates religion with being a good, moral person.
- Therapeutic equates faith to feeling better about oneself.
- Deism is a belief that God exists, but He's not involved in people's daily affairs.[16]

Faith is not a distant God Who wants you to be a good person so you feel good about yourself. That sounds selfish. And how do you know if you're good enough to feel good about yourself?

Could faith be different from what we think it is?

WHAT FAITH IS

So, what is faith? You won't be overwhelmed by what it is, but genuine faith is profound and life-changing.

Faith is trust.

Trust is the difference between sitting on the edge of a chair or sitting back in a chair. When you sit on the edge of a chair, you're ready if it breaks. You won't fall. Your feet are firmly planted on the ground, and your weight is still on your legs and feet, just in case.

When you sit back in a chair, you fully trust that chair to hold you. You're all in. If the chair breaks, your whole body ends up on the ground. That's trust!

I believe everyone has faith in something or someone. You may be aware of who or what you trust. You may not be aware. I know some people say they do not have faith, but I disagree. You trust something. You put your faith in:

- financial account balances
- sports teams
- plans
- traditions
- other people
- a job

- promises made
- a church
- possessions
- a goal
- yourself
- politicians
- the past
- rules
- _____ (fill in the blank with what / who you tend to trust)

When you put your faith in these things, you trust them for desired outcomes. It could be something tangible. Maybe a feeling. It's trusting you will get what you want and think you deserve. That is not how faith works.

How is faith meant to work?

Faith is not meant to be fragile and temporary. Faith is meant to be dependable and eternal. When you trust the one person, the only person you can truly put your faith in, you receive a new life. You become a new person. Faith is not a part of your life; it is your new life. It is how you live...how you think, talk, act, etc. Paul, in Acts 17:28, used a philosopher's words to describe this new life only found in faith in Jesus: *"For in him we live and move and have our being."*

Paul, a man who trusted so many things before he trusted Jesus, wrote in 2 Corinthians 5:17, "*Therefore, if anyone is in Christ, the new creation has come: The old has gone, the new is here!*" And in Galatians 2:20, he wrote, "*I have been crucified with Christ and I no longer live, but Christ lives in me. The life I now live in the body, I live by faith in the Son of God, who loved me and gave himself for me.*"

FAITH IN JESUS

Paul experienced the difference between trusting himself, achievements, religion, rules, etc., and trusting Jesus. He could write about the new life found in putting your faith in Jesus because he experienced it first-hand.

Faith in Jesus is trusting his death and resurrection to save you from all the things you do that separate you from God. Sin. Backward steps.

Before you start your faith, your sin separates you from God. When you begin your faith, you are reconciled to God, and your broken relationship is now repaired and healthy. You're even called a child of God. John wrote in John 1:12-13, "*Yet to all who did receive him, to those who believed in his name, he gave the right to become children of God – children born not of natural descent, nor of human decision or a husband's will, but born of God.*"

Faith in Jesus is trusting Jesus with your entire past, present, and future. Everything is at stake. And he is the one person you can trust with your whole life. When you decide to put your faith in Jesus, your life changes, you may not feel different, and life will still be complicated, but your life is new. You are a new person.

When you put your faith in Jesus, you find:

- Peace for your soul
- Forgiveness for your sins
- Hope for your life[17]

The most significant decision in your life is to start your faith in Jesus.

If you have not started your faith in Jesus and want to do that right now, you can. John wrote in John 3:16-17, *"For God so loved the world that he gave his one and only Son, that whoever believes in him shall not perish but have eternal life. For God did not send his Son into the world to condemn the world, but to save the world through him."*

GOD LOVED

God loves you. That statement should blow our minds. What could we do to earn God's love? Nothing. He chooses to love you and me.

GOD GAVE

When someone loves someone else, what do they do? They give the other person all they can. God gave you His Son Jesus by sacrificing him for your good.

YOU BELIEVE

What should your response be to God loving you and giving you Jesus? You trust. You believe so much in Jesus dying for you and rising from the dead that you put your faith in Jesus.

YOU RECEIVE[18]

God does not force Jesus on you. And you do not inherit Jesus from your family, church, country, or anyone else. You must choose to start your faith in Jesus.

If you want to start your faith in Jesus, trust what Jesus did for you and pray something like this:

"Today, Jesus, I trust you. Before today, I trusted so many other things and people. I did so many things that separated me from God. Thank you for forgiving me. Help me to trust you from now on. Help me to live like you and for you from this day forward. Thank you for loving me and giving me a way to live with you forever. I put my trust in you and will take steps to trust you more for the rest of my life."

I think you'll agree with what Paul wrote in Romans 3:23, *"for all have sinned and fall short of the glory of God."* I don't deserve the freedom to put my faith in Jesus. I'm not good enough. I know too much about myself. It is incredible that we even get the opportunity to start our faith in Jesus.

But Paul also wrote in Romans 3:22-25, *"This righteousness is given through faith in Jesus Christ to all who believe. There is no difference between Jew and Gentile, for all have sinned and fall short of the glory of God, and all are justified freely by his grace through the redemption that came by Christ Jesus. God presented Christ as a sacrifice of atonement, through the shedding of his blood - to be received by faith."*

The righteousness you can receive through Jesus dying for your sins happens when you put your trust in Jesus. Your faith in Jesus changes everything.

You've started your faith in Jesus. Now what?

I believe the Bible has two expectations of your faith in Jesus. Jesus and the writers of the New Testament expected your faith to 1) consistently mature and 2) consistently be active.

MORE MATURE FAITH

I think we get maturity all wrong. Please allow me to present my case.

EXHIBIT ONE: OUR EDUCATION SYSTEM

We give kids credit for being mature every August or September. They accumulated enough "good enough" test scores the previous school year, so we advance them to the next grade. They are now more mature because they're in a new grade.

Are they truly more mature? Maybe. Maybe not. But we give a 9th-grade boy credit for being more mature than an 8th-grade boy because he is in a higher grade. Do you know any real-life 9th-grade boys? I do. Yes, some are more mature than 8th-grade boys, but some are less mature than 4th-grade boys. (I am not even kidding.)

We give kids credit for being mature when they advance to a new grade, but we know this is not real maturity. There is more to it.

EXHIBIT TWO: THE NEIGHBORHOOD SWIMMING POOL

The neighborhood swimming pool is an amazing place. And by "amazing" I mean a shocking social experiment.

We typically give adults credit for being mature when they have a job, get married, have a kid, invest some money, plan for retirement, buy a home... things like that. But have you spent any time with adults at the neighborhood swimming pool?

I have. It's like a reality TV show gone bad.

Instead of acting like the mature adults we give them credit for being, they act like they're back in college. And not the study-to-get-a-degree-to-get-a-job college experience. The party-like-there-are-no-consequences college experience.

With their kids playing in the pool, these adults get drunk, flirt, say embarrassing things, brag about themselves, and act like they're the most important people on the planet.

I know you don't act like this. I'm talking about "those" people.

We give them credit for being mature, but we know this is not true maturity. There is more to it.

EXHIBIT THREE: MOST CHRISTIANS

If you've been around the church long, you know Christians love knowledge and information, especially hard-to-understand knowledge. Sometimes the more complex something is to understand, the more Christians love it. They often feel the need to defend the knowledge they know. The people with the most knowledge are usually placed on a pedestal reserved for the best Christians.

Those who know the most must live the best, right? Nope. We know there is more to being a mature Christian than knowledge.

Jesus opposed the people who valued knowledge over faith. Matthew wrote in Matthew 23:25-28, "'Woe to you, teachers of the law and Pharisees, you hypocrites! You clean the outside of the cup and dish, but inside they are full of greed and self-indulgence. Blind Pharisee! First clean the inside of the cup and dish, and then the outside also will be clean.

Woe to you, teachers of the law and Pharisees, you hypocrites! You are like whitewashed tombs, which look beautiful on the outside but on the inside are full of the bones of the dead and everything unclean. In the same way, on the outside you appear to people as righteous but on the inside you are full of hypocrisy and wickedness.'"

In First Corinthians 8:1-3, Paul wrote, "Now about food sacrificed to idols: We know that 'We all possess knowledge.' But knowledge puffs up while love builds up. Those who think they know something do not yet know as they ought to know. But whoever loves God is known by God."

Knowledge is important when it comes to your faith in Jesus, but it does not automatically result in maturity. And it doesn't even result in more faith. More knowledge just results in knowing more.

Correct thinking is important. Believing correctly about God, Jesus, and His teachings is important. Knowing the Bible is important. However, knowledge accumulation is not the same as mature faith. Knowledge was never meant to be the goal.

Maybe more Christian knowledge is not your thing. Maybe your thing is more intense emotions when it comes to your faith. Some Christians want to feel closer and closer to God. What does that even mean?

You attend every night of worship, go on every mission trip, raise your hands higher when you sing, and meet with every mentor to feel closer to God. You look for the highs and lows with your faith because it's in those times you feel God. Feelings do not lead to maturity.

Feeling close to God is not the goal. Feelings were never meant to be the goal.

Faith is the goal. Trusting Jesus more and more is the goal.

When knowledge leads to greater lived-out trust in Jesus, your faith matures. When emotions lead to greater lived-out trust in Jesus, your faith matures.

If age, life goals, grades, knowledge, and emotions do not achieve maturity, what does? Growing up achieves maturity.

Maturity is the natural progress of anything healthy. It happens all around you. Living things...human and in nature...mature. They progress in the right direction if they are healthy.

Stephen R. Covey, in *The 7 Habits of Highly Effective People* (One of my top five books of all time.), explained maturity beautifully: "On the maturity continuum, dependence is the paradigm of you – you take care of me; you come through for me; you didn't come through; I blame you for the results.

Independence is the paradigm of I – I can do it; I am responsible; I am self-reliant; I can choose.

Interdependence is the paradigm of we – we can do it; we can cooperate; we can combine our talents and abilities and create something greater together."[19]

As you'll see, I believe his explanation fits all humans, especially those who have started their faith in Jesus.

How do you respond when you see a baby drinking from a bottle? Cute, right? How would you react if you saw an adult drinking from a baby bottle? Creepy, right? The writer of Hebrews used natural maturity to explain our faith in Jesus. He knew we'd understand if he compared a baby's eating habits to an adult's. The writer wrote in Hebrews 5:12 through 6:1, *"In fact, though by this time you ought to be teachers, you need someone to teach you the elementary truths of God's word all over again. You need milk, not solid food! Anyone who lives on milk, being still an infant, is not acquainted with the teaching about righteousness. But solid food is for the mature, who by constant use have trained themselves to distinguish good from evil.*

Therefore let us move beyond the elementary teachings about Christ and be taken forward to maturity, not laying again the foundation of repentance from acts that lead to death, and of faith in God,..."

Even thousands of years ago, there was a problem with adults not growing up. Maturity has always been a problem regarding our faith in Jesus.

In 1 Corinthians 13:11, Paul wrote, *"When I was a child, I talked like a child, I thought like a child, I reasoned like a child. When I became a man, I put the ways of childhood behind me."*

What would you think if you saw a grown-up stomp their feet, scream, fall on the ground, and cry when they did not get what they wanted? That video would go viral. It would be so ridiculous. I'd watch that.

Think about your own life. What do you do today that you did the same way as when you were in first grade? Or ten years ago? You've matured. You've grown up. You are growing up. Like you were meant to do.

What does a faith in Jesus that is growing up look like?

YOU ARE KNOWN AND NEEDED

I believe we all have a basic human desire to be known and needed. You want others to make moves to know and need you. You feel loved and valued when others know and need you.

And Christians should feel more known and needed than any other group. In 1 Corinthians 12:1-26, Paul wrote so clearly and creatively, *"Now about the gifts of the Spirit, brothers and sisters, I do not want you to be uninformed. You know that when you were pagans, you were somehow influenced and led astray to mute idols. Therefore I want you to know that no one who is speaking by the Spirit of God says, 'Jesus be cursed,' and no one can say, 'Jesus is Lord,' except by the Holy Spirit.*

There are different kinds of gifts, but the same Spirit distributes them. There are different kinds of service, but the same Lord. There are different kinds of working, but in all of them and in everyone it is the same God at work.

Now to each one the manifestation of the Spirit is given for the common good. To one there is given through the Spirit a message of wisdom, to another a message of knowledge by means of the same Spirit, to another faith by the same Spirit, to another gifts of healing by that one Spirit, to another miraculous powers, to another prophecy, to another distinguishing between spirits, to another speaking in different kinds of tongues, and to still another the interpretation of tongues. All these are the work of one and the same Spirit, and he distributes them to each one, just as he determines.

Just as a body, though one, has many parts, but all its many parts form one body, so it is with Christ. For we were all baptized by one Spirit so as to form one body – whether Jews or Gentiles, slave or free – and we were all given the one Spirit to drink. Even so the body is not made up of one part but of many.

Now if the foot should say, 'Because I am not a hand, I do not belong to the body,' it would not for that reason stop being part of the body. And if the ear should say, 'Because I am not an eye, I do not belong to the body,' it would not for that reason stop being part of the body. Where would the sense of hearing be if the whole body were an eye? If the whole body were an ear, where would the sense of smell be? But in fact God has placed the parts in the body, every one of them, just as he wanted them to be. If they were all one part, where would the body be? As it is, there are many parts, but one body.

The eye cannot say to the hand, 'I don't need you!' And the head cannot say to the feet, 'I don't need you!' On the contrary, those parts of the body that seem to be weaker are indispensable, and the parts that we think are less honorable we treat with special honor. And the parts that are unpresentable are treated with special modesty, while our presentable parts need no special treatment. But God has put the body together, giving greater honor to the parts that lacked it, so that there should be no division in the body, but that its parts should have equal concern for each other. If one part suffers, every part suffers with it; if one part is honored, every part rejoices with it."

Christians are the most needed people on the planet. When you start your faith in Jesus, you instantly become part of his church, his movement, and his plan to change the world. You play a specific role in it. You are needed so the church functions as it is designed to function.

Your faith makes you a significant part of something bigger than you.

The church is not perfect. It will disappoint you. It's led by people trying their best. But the church is still the thing Jesus established to reach the world. In Matthew 16:17-18, *"Jesus replied, 'Blessed are you, Simon son of Jonah, for this was not revealed to you by flesh and blood, but by my Father in heaven. And I tell you that you are Peter, and on this rock I will build my church, and the gates of Hades will not overcome it.'"*

People becoming more mature in their faith in Jesus are making themselves more known and needed in their church. They should always be asking themselves: How am I doing my part for my church?

You're not waiting to be asked to be needed. You're humbly meeting needs in the church, so it functions as it is supposed to work. You're known and needed because you're raising your hand to serve, not because the church is coming to you, and not because they have the perfect spot for you.

YOU ARE READY

A mature faith in Jesus means you are ready for what's next. What's next? I don't know. You can't know. Life is complicated. There is some good stuff coming. There is some bad stuff coming. There is some significant and insignificant stuff coming. "Stuff" seems like a good word to use.

Whatever is coming will have the ability to sway your faith in Jesus.

Paul wrote in Ephesians 4:12-16, *"...so that the body of Christ may be built up until we all reach unity in the faith and in the knowledge of the Son of God and become mature, attaining to the whole measure of the fullness of Christ.*

Then we will no longer be infants, tossed back and forth by the waves, and blown here and there by every wind of teaching and by the cunning and craftiness of people in their deceitful scheming. Instead, speaking the truth in love, we will grow to become in every respect the mature body of him who is the head, that is, Christ. From him the whole body, joined and held together by every supporting ligament, grows and builds itself up in love, as each part does its work."

Can you confidently say, **"My faith makes me ready for life and relation- ships."**? A person who has faith in Jesus should be able to say this with confidence. A faith that is consistently maturing causes you to be ready for what is coming in your life. Is your faith growing up? Are you more and more ready for life the longer you're a Christian?

There are specific things you can do to make yourself more ready. As you do these things, your faith matures, making you more and more ready for what's next in this complicated life.

Within your church, you can:

- serve where the greatest need is
- participate in a group Bible study
- get baptized
- mentor someone
- participate in worship services

Outside your church, you can:

- see a counselor
- do personal Bible study
- pray
- read books
- have faith-growing conversations

· share your story with others

Jesus and the writers of the New Testament expected your faith to mature consistently. Your faith is supposed to grow up. They also expected our faith to be always active. "Active" and "activity" are not the same thing.

MORE ACTIVE FAITH

Have you ever met someone who is an expert on teenagers, and they have never parented anyone over the age of twelve? Parents, how do these people make you feel? Like throwing something at them? Like laughing hysterically at anything they say? Like letting them be responsible for your kids for one week? Just me? You're probably much nicer than me. These people bother you, right?

Action gives credibility to a person's words and beliefs. Your actions of parenting a teenager give you the credibility to talk about parenting teenagers. Without action, your words mean less, no matter how loudly you yell or how smart you sound. James, the brother of Jesus, wrote in James 2:14-19, *"What good is it, my brothers and sisters, if someone claims to have faith but has no deeds? Can such faith save them? Suppose a brother or a sister is without clothes and daily food. If one of you says to them, 'Go in peace; keep warm and well fed,' but does nothing about their physical needs, what good is it? In the same way, faith by itself, if it is not accompanied by action, is dead.*

But someone will say, 'You have faith; I have deeds.' Show me your faith without deeds, and I will show you my faith by my deeds. You believe that there is one God. Good! Even the demons believe that – and shudder."

One of the interesting things about faith in Jesus is even people who have not put their trust in Jesus know there should be actions that go with this kind of faith. People who have not put their faith in Jesus may look down on faith in Jesus, but they expect people with faith in Jesus to act a certain way.

Christians are great at Christian activity. You love to be busy doing Christian activities, but that is not what I mean by "active" and not what those without faith in Jesus look for from you.

Christians are also experts at acting good and not acting badly. That's basic ethics. And again, that is not what I mean by "active" and not what those without faith in Jesus are looking for from you.

Active faith is trusting Jesus more by doing what needs to be done. What should your active faith in Jesus look like?

DO WHAT NEEDS TO BE DONE

Faith in Jesus changes how you live your life. You act differently than you did before you put your trust in Jesus. You act differently than people who have not put their faith in Jesus. Faith results in the right actions. Just in case you need a reminder, love is always the right thing to do and what needs to be done.

People who have put their faith in Jesus have the ultimate advantage. You have the Holy Spirit, God Himself, inside of you. In 2 Corinthians 1:21-22, Paul wrote, *"Now it is God who makes both us and you stand firm in Christ. He anointed us, set his seal of ownership on us, and put his Spirit in our hearts as a deposit, guaranteeing what is to come."*

In Ephesians 1:13-14, he wrote, *"And you also were included in Christ when you heard the message of truth, the gospel of your salvation. When you believed, you were marked in him with a seal, the promised Holy Spirit, who is a deposit guaranteeing our inheritance until the redemption of those who are God's possession - to the praise of his glory."*

With the Holy Spirit in you, you have God in you, helping you live the right kind of active faith in this complicated life.

What does the right kind of active faith look like?

In Galatians 5:22-25, Paul said a person who has the Holy Spirit in them would exhibit specific actions. *"But the fruit of the Spirit is love, joy, peace, forbearance, kindness, goodness, faithfulness, gentleness and self-control. Against such things there is no law. Those who belong to Christ Jesus have crucified the flesh with its passions and desires. Since we live by the Spirit, let us keep in step with the Spirit."*

Love – Joy – Peace – Forbearance (Patience) – Kindness –
Goodness – Faithfulness – Gentleness – Self-Control

Since the Holy Spirit is in you, these actions should be observed more and more in your life as you grow up and are more active. These are the right things to do. These things show love to others.

An active faith does not make God love you more. An active faith does not make you closer to God. Matthew, after he started his faith in Jesus, wrote in Matthew 5:14-16 the result of active faith, *"You are the light of the world. A town built on a hill cannot be hidden. Neither do people light a lamp and put it under a bowl. Instead, they put it on its stand, and it gives light to everyone in the house. In the same way, let your light shine before others, that they may see your good deeds and glorify your Father in heaven."*

Your active faith results in others putting their attention on God. **Faith in Jesus leads you to do the right thing for others.** Does this describe your faith?

Peter Scazzero wrote, "Jesus refused to accept that people were growing in love for God in a way that did not translate into love for people. We must refuse to accept that as well. The religious leaders of his day knew their Bible, practiced spiritual disciplines, and worshipped faithfully, but they were defensive, judgmental, and unsafe to be around."[20]

Doing the right thing for others should happen within the church, but it *needs* to happen outside of it, too. How? The possibilities are limitless. Well, maybe there's a limit at some point, but none of us will get there.

Doing the right thing for others outside the church could look like:

- repair a damaged relationship
- deal with a habit or addiction
- volunteer in a local organization
- start a new job
- start a new friendship
- support a local business
- meet someone's physical needs
- be generous to someone
- join your HOA
- help someone else succeed
- work less
- make sure your family feels loved by you
- express joy for those you are thankful for
- be patient with a difficult person
- show kindness to a stranger
- do good to someone for no reason
- coach a local sports team
- be trustworthy to someone who needs you
- be gentle to someone who is hurting
- show self-control in a situation

What needs to be done in any situation and any relationship? The right thing needs to be done. And when your faith is active, you can do the right thing more and more.

EXPERIENCE MOMENTUM

An active faith not only does the right thing but also experiences momentum.

I love all five seasons of the calendar year: winter, spring, summer, fall, and March Madness. You experience March Madness, right? I never win our family's bracket challenge, but I love that time of the year. So much meaningful college basketball: The brackets. The upsets. The stories. It hits me just like watching the leaves change colors in the Georgia mountains.

A team's success during March Madness has so much to do with momentum. As someone famously called it, "the big mo!" A team with "the big mo" is on a roll. They are difficult to defeat. They are working hard, and things just seem to go their way. And they win!

This is what an active faith in Jesus looks like. When your faith in Jesus is active, you experience momentum. **You'll feel momentum when your faith compels you to help others start their faith.**

In 2 Corinthians 5:17-21, Paul wrote. *"Therefore, if anyone is in Christ, the new creation has come: The old has gone, the new is here! All this is from God, who reconciled us to himself through Christ and gave us the ministry of reconciliation: that God was reconciling the world to himself in Christ, not counting people's sins against them. And he has committed to us the message of reconciliation. We are therefore Christ's ambassadors, as though God were making his appeal through us. We implore you on Christ's behalf: Be reconciled to God. God made him who had no sin to be sin for us, so that in him we might become the righteousness of God."*

When you start your faith in Jesus, God gives you a purpose. Is anyone looking for their purpose? When you live out His purpose for you, you experience momentum. When you do not live out His purpose for you, you do not experience momentum in your faith. Yes, it's that simple.

Our purpose is to show and tell others that Jesus came to reconcile them to God. You can share how Jesus reconciled you to God and how that has affected your life. You can share this with words and with actions.

How are you influencing others to start their faith? Here are some ideas:

- go to a church that is easy to invite people to
- go public with your faith through baptism
- look for local organizations that allow you to be active with your faith
- share your story with others
- give people a clear opportunity to start their faith in Jesus

Active faith in Jesus is a faith that experiences momentum. Faith that experiences momentum is a faith that is helping others start their faith in Jesus.

WHAT NOW?

I can't move on without saying this: If you have not started your faith in Jesus, please do that now. Will life get better? Maybe. Will you get better at life? Yes. Will those around you be better because of your decision? Yes. And you will have this for the rest of your life:

- Peace for your soul

- Forgiveness for your sins
- Hope for your life

Your faith is your faith. It is not your parent's faith. It is not your church's faith. It is not your pastor's faith. Each one of these things may have influenced your faith in some very positive ways, but your faith is your faith. It is your responsibility.

So...how is your faith in Jesus right now?

I genuinely want you to be able to say confidently:

- My faith makes me a significant part of something bigger than me...my church.
- My faith makes me ready for life and relationships.
- My faith leads me to do the right thing.
- My faith compels me to help others start their faith.

As a way to check up on how you're doing, ask yourself:

- How am I doing my part for my church?
- How am I making myself ready for what's next?
- How am I doing the right thing for others?
- How am I influencing others to start their faith?

CONVERSATION QUESTIONS

What wrong definitions of faith have you believed?

What are some fragile, temporary things you've put your faith in? What outcomes were you hoping for?

When and why did you start your faith in Jesus?

Is your faith in Jesus consistently more mature? Why did you answer that way?

Is your faith in Jesus consistently more active? Why did you answer that way?

9

THIS IS IT? (WHEN LIFE AND FAITH FEEL DISAPPOINTING)

I am lyrically challenged. Are you aware of this disorder? I just made it up.

I legit do not know the correct words to a single song. I *think* I know the right words to just about every song, but I do not. Do you know someone like me?

My challenge is highlighted by the fact that I love many kinds of music. Hip hop. Country. Top 40. The 80s. The 90s. The 2000s. Rap. Pop. Musicals. Alternative rock. K-pop. Worship.

I even sing the wrong words to worship songs. Yes, I'm a pastor. Yes, even when the words are displayed on a large screen so everyone can know the correct words, I get them wrong.

I am genuinely surprised when I find out the correct words to any song.

My family catches me singing the wrong words all the time. Mostly because I like to sing loud around them. I often hear a random word, and a song pops into my mind. So, I start singing (incorrectly), of course. They enjoy catching me singing the wrong lyrics - they enjoy it too much. Something is wrong with them.

If I am being honest, I disappoint myself regarding lyrics. I genuinely want to get the lyrics right. I sing the wrong lyrics with passion. When the music plays, and the volume turns up, the wrong words just come out. I'm not trying to be funny. The correct words just don't come out.

THIS IS IT?

You've read this far, so I feel like we're friends, and I can confess something to you. I hope it's okay to tell you this. It may be a little disturbing because I'm a pastor, but I trust you.

If I am honest, I also disappoint myself regarding my faith in Jesus. I genuinely want to have a meaningful, thriving faith all the time. I want people to watch me and say, "Wow! Your faith in Jesus is so awesome. You trust Jesus for everything. I want what you have." It just doesn't happen all the time...maybe hardly ever.

I'm not talking about Bible study, attending an awesome church, praying, doing life with some guys who love Jesus, praying with my family, etc. I do all that...most of the time. I do the faith activities well. I'm a pastor. It's kind of my job. You know what I mean.

Something tells me there is more to faith than a list of to-dos. The Bible tells me that too. My life is supposed to look and feel radically different than those who have not put their faith in Jesus. My life should regularly result in outcomes only God can do because God's Spirit is inside me, and I trust Jesus more and more. Not because I am a pastor. Because I have put my faith in Jesus...I am a Christian. I can't help but wonder when I look at reality, "This is it?"

Lean in so no one else hears me say this to you. Make sure no one else is listening. It feels like my faith is more about me and what I do than trusting Jesus in our complicated world. This is where I hope you say, "Me too."

I'm usually most concerned about what I need, what my family needs, what needs to happen at work, what I want to happen, etc. I care the most about myself, my world, and my family. I don't care enough about trusting Jesus more and more. You too, right? Please say "yes" so I am not alone.

Is it okay to admit your faith in Jesus feels disappointing? Yes. How do you admit this? Say it with me: "God, my faith in Jesus feels disappointing." I believe saying these words can be the catalyst for experiencing a thriving faith.

Is God going to get mad at you for acknowledging your faith in His Son feels disappointing? No. God does not love you any less, even though your faith in Jesus disappoints you. God is not a human. He does not think, act, react, etc., as we do. That's a relief.

In Romans 8:31-39, Paul wrote, *"What, then, shall we say in response to these things? If God is for us, who can be against us? He who did not spare his own Son, but gave him up for us all - how will he not also, along with him, graciously give us all things? Who will bring any charge against those whom God has chosen? It is God who justifies. Who then is the one who condemns? No one. Christ Jesus who died - more than that, who was raised to life - is at the right hand of God and is also interceding for us. Who shall separate us from the love of Christ? Shall trouble, hardship, persecution, famine, nakedness, danger, or sword? As it is written:*

'For your sake we face death all day long; we are considered as sheep to be slaughtered.'

No, in all these things we are more than conquerors through him who loved us. For I am convinced that neither death nor life, neither angels nor demons, neither the present nor the future, nor any powers, neither height nor depth, nor anything else in all creation, will be able to separate us from the love of God that is in Christ Jesus our Lord."

Julie, Bennett, Canon, Teague, Casey, and _____ (insert your name), God loves you and is not disappointed in you. Yes, He does want more for you through your faith in Jesus. He knows life is complicated. He does not want you to have a disappointing life. He wants you to take steps forward. He wants you to stop asking, "This is it?"

SIGNS YOUR FAITH MAY BE DISAPPOINTING

I realize not everyone can relate to this part of the book. Some of you have remarkable faith in Jesus. You trust Jesus more and more each day. Others notice your faith and are drawn to start their faith in Jesus. I'm high-fiving you! I'm jealous of you.

For many of us, though, there's something that tells us our faith in Jesus should do more, mean more, matter more, and result in more, but we keep doing the same things and getting the same results. We must stop.

See if you can relate to these common signs of disappointing faith:

- You rarely do things that take courage.
- You believe everything you think about God is correct.

- You're doing the same thing to grow your faith as you were one year ago.
- There is not much difference between your life and the life of your friend who has not put their faith in Jesus.
- You commonly look down on other Christians.
- Your faith does not feel like an adventure.
- You don't feel close to God.
- No one is asking you about the trust in Jesus you're displaying.
- You commonly look down on other people.
- You spend more time learning about faith than living out your faith.

The most common sign of disappointing faith is when your goal in life is to have your feet firmly planted on the ground. Have you noticed Christians celebrate and thank God for an easy life? But your trust in Jesus rarely grows in these times. Your words and actions should cause you to take steps to increase your trust in Jesus. Instead, you often do everything you can to stand still with your feet firmly planted. You must stop.

WHY YOUR FAITH FEELS DISAPPOINTING

How do you usually respond when your faith is not what you want it to be? If you're like most people, you increase your activity. You join a small group, go on a mission trip, start volunteering, or something like that. Your faith may feel better for a moment or a season, but it returns to disappointing. The kind of faith you're looking for is not found in church activity.

It's usually not too challenging to figure out why your faith keeps you wondering, "This is it?" Here are some typical reasons I've observed in my own life. Maybe you can relate?

LIFE IS COMPLICATED

We talked all about life earlier in the book. Even on your very best days, life is complicated. This is true for everyone. A complicated life causes your faith in Jesus to often feel disappointing. Isn't faith supposed to fix everything? No. When it doesn't, we're disappointed.

EXPECTATIONS

The first step is admitting you have a problem, right?

Okay. Here it goes. Hello, my name is Casey, and I have a problem. I have a few, but one relates to this chapter. My problem is my expectations.

It's a real problem. It's one of those problems that causes a multitude, a plethora, a whole bunch of other problems. My wife Julie is shouting "Amen!" right now...if she's read this far. She gets to witness or be on the other side of most of the issues my expectations cause. I'm sorry, Julie.

Fortunately for those around me, most of my expectations remain in my mind. I don't say them out loud, but I expect other people and situations to live up to what I want them to do. And very few do. It's not their fault.

Peter Bregman (CEO, author, and speaker) says, "High expectations can have a positive effect; people need a high bar to stretch towards. But I think many of us take it too far. We slip so easily into criticisms of ourselves and those around us — family, friends, coworkers, public figures — that we no longer expect people to be human beings. And when we shame ourselves and others for failing, we make things worse. We contribute to pain while nurturing impotence."[21]

Ouch! That hurts. I take expectations too far. I hope you don't. It's not a fun way to live...for me or those around me.

You have expectations of your faith. You have expectations of God. You have expectations of your church. Have you spent time thinking about your expectations of these things? You should. They're likely not meeting your expectations because they are too high and unrealistic, and this impacts your faith in Jesus a lot.

UNANSWERED PRAYERS

Have you ever prayed for something, and God did not do what you wanted Him to do? Of course, you have. I have hundreds of times. Maybe thousands of times. Honestly, some of my prayers He did not answer were silly and insignificant. But other times, what I was praying for was a big deal. I prayed hard for our church in Greenville to stay open, but I eventually had to stand on the stage and announce we were closing. That was tough.

I don't know why He did not answer my prayers as I wanted Him to. Sometimes I felt disappointed. Other times I was angry or confused. It can be challenging to trust when you don't get what you want.

THE FUTURE

The future causes all sorts of disappointments in our life, including disappointment when it comes to our faith in Jesus. You cannot know the future. You cannot control the future. You want your future to look a certain way. You want certain people in your future. You want your faith to make your future better, but life just does not cooperate. And that affects how we feel about our faith in Jesus.

YOUR FAITH

When you define "faith" the wrong way, your faith in Jesus can cause you to feel disappointed in your faith in Jesus. Hopefully, chapter six helped you define "faith" in a way that helps you have fulfilling faith. Remember, your faith should be consistently maturing and consistently active. If you cannot say these things with confidence, your faith will feel disappointing:

- My faith makes me a significant part of something bigger than me...my church.
- My faith makes me ready for life and relationships.
- My faith leads me to do the right thing.
- My faith compels me to help others start their faith.

SUCCESS

Success is a funny thing. You love it. You crave it. You celebrate it. And when it happens, you often trust Jesus less. And when you trust Jesus less, your faith disappoints you. Success eventually disappears, and when it does, you wonder why your faith feels like, "This is it?"

FEELINGS

Have you ever paid attention to how much you measure your faith in Jesus by your feelings? When you feel close to God, your faith is strong; when you feel moved by the music, your faith is strong. When you do something you want to do or are good at, you feel close to God. And the opposite is true. You feel disappointed in your faith when you don't like the music. When you face a challenge, you feel far from God. Feelings are never the measure of your faith in Jesus. Your level of trust is the only measure of your faith.

OTHER CHRISTIANS

This one can hurt a little extra. Other people who have put their faith in Jesus hurt your faith in Jesus. This happens way too often. They hurt you. They discourage you. They let you down. And your faith in Jesus feels disappointing. Shouldn't they be different? Yes. Shouldn't they build you up instead of letting you down? Yes.

They are people, like you and me, hopefully trying their best to live out their faith in Jesus in this complicated life. I'm not excusing their words or actions that hurt you. It hurts when you take a hit from someone on your own team.

WRONG THINKING

A.W. Tozer wrote, "What comes into our minds when we think about God is the most important thing about us."[22] I love this quote and have seen how right he is over and over in my own life and the lives of others. The problem is no one thinks 100% correctly about God.

Your theology is what you believe about God. I hate to be the one to break it to you, but your theology is not perfect. My theology is not perfect, and I have a master's degree in theology. And the real problem is we do not know where our theology is wrong. It's just not possible for you to think 100% correctly about God. You are not capable of it.

Isaiah wrote in Isaiah 55:8-9, "'For my thoughts are not your thoughts, neither are your ways my ways,' declares the Lord. 'As the heavens are higher than the earth, so are my ways higher than your ways and my thoughts than your thoughts.'"

Paul wrote in Romans 11:33-34, "Oh, the depth of the riches of the wisdom and knowledge of God! How unsearchable his judgments, and his paths beyond tracing out! Who has known the mind of the Lord? Or who has been his counselor?"

Tozer also wrote, "Left to ourselves we tend immediately to reduce God to manageable terms. We want to get Him where we can use Him, or at least know where He is when we need Him. We want a God we can in some measure control. We need the feeling of security that comes from knowing what God is like, and what He is like is a composite of all the religious pictures we have seen, all the best people we have known or heard about, and all the sublime ideas we have entertained."[23]

We must be humble enough to admit we have some incorrect thoughts about God. And your wrong thinking about God causes you to feel disappointed in your faith.

BAD CHURCH EXPERIENCE

There are whole books and podcasts about this topic. If you've ever attended church, you have probably been disappointed by the pastor, music, policies, etc. People lead the church, and people let you down all the time. And when those people are attached to a church, the disappointment can be painful and affect your faith.

FEAR

And we have a winner! I believe fear is the number one reason people have a disappointing faith in Jesus. It's my top reason. Soon, we will dive deep into why fear affects your faith so much. For now, it's enough to acknowledge that fear prevents you from trusting Jesus with your whole life. It prevents you from taking forward steps in life. Fear is why you prefer and pray to stand still in life.

I've heard others say that the phrase "fear not" or similar expressions are in the Bible over 300 times. I don't think the exact number matters. What matters is God knows you well. He knows you have a natural tendency to get scared. So, He makes sure to tell you repeatedly not to be afraid.

One of my favorite places in the Bible where He does this is in Joshua. Joshua is about to lead a large group of people to accomplish something significant. He has been talking to these people and is about to move forward. Remember, life is words and actions.

Just before he takes a step forward, we read in Joshua 1:7-9, *"Be strong and very courageous. Be careful to obey all the law my servant Moses gave you; do not turn from it to the right or to the left, that you may be successful wherever you go. Keep this Book of the Law always on your lips; meditate on it day and night, so that you may be careful to do everything written in it. Then you will be prosperous and successful. Have I not commanded you? Be strong and courageous. Do not be afraid; do not be discouraged, for the Lord your God will be with you wherever you go."*

You do not tell someone, "be strong" or "be courageous" if he or she is feeling strong and courageous. You tell someone, "do not be afraid" when he or she feels afraid. It is normal for you to experience fear, but you need to understand your fear causes your faith to feel disappointing.

WHAT YOU DO WHEN YOUR FAITH DISAPPOINTS YOU

Sometimes you're willing to admit your faith feels disappointing. Other times, you're not aware you're feeling disappointed by your faith. Regardless of how much you're aware of it, you act out in specific ways that tell you your faith feels disappointing. See if any of these responses sound familiar.

BLAME

When your faith feels disappointing, you find something to blame. You blame the church. You blame a pastor. You blame your favorite sports team. You blame God. You blame your spouse. You blame the songs sung at church. You blame traffic. You blame sermons. You blame the volume of the songs at church. You blame the temperature of the church. You will blame just about anything or anyone.

Believe it or not, I've heard all the above responses regarding placing blame for your disappointing faith. You love to blame. It makes you feel like whatever you're feeling is not your fault. You get in a blame loop and forget there is something you can do about it.

WALK AWAY

This response is the one that breaks my heart the most. You walk away from God, people, and the church when you feel let down by your faith. Of course, you can't walk away from God, but you try to.

I get it. You're disappointed in something that is supposed to be the most important and meaningful thing in your life. Why stick around for more hurt and frustration? But faith is trust. Trust only happens when you take the risk to trust.

TAKE CONTROL

When my faith in Jesus feels disappointing, I take control. I tell myself I am taking over. I put my head down and start doing what I believe will get me what I want.

Faith in Jesus is difficult for people like me. I trust myself. I know what I am going to do. Faith in Jesus means trusting someone else with every part of my life, and I cannot even see Jesus! That does not come naturally for someone like me. So, when my faith in Jesus disappoints me, I quickly take control and get busy trying to make things do what I want them to do.

SEEK THE SHALLOW END

Seeking the shallow end is our natural tendency when life feels disappointing. You intentionally seek the shallow end when you start asking, "This is it?" as it relates to your faith in Jesus. When both feet are firmly planted on the bottom, you feel safe. Trust is challenging. It's ok to admit that. So, when trusting Jesus feels like it's not working, you seek what is easy.

FEEL SHAME

Shame shows up when life feels complicated. Shame also shows up when your faith in Jesus feels disappointing. You think to yourself: "I'm a terrible person. I can't even trust Jesus, right? How could God accept or love me if my faith feels disappointing?"

Those are lies. You deserve love and acceptance no matter what. Whether your faith is thriving or disappointing, you are loved and accepted by God.

EVEN THEY HAD DISAPPOINTING FAITH

Admitting my faith in Jesus feels disappointing is not a scary thing to me. Life is complicated, and I am not perfect.

A significant reason I'm okay admitting my faith feels disappointing at times is that I've read about Jesus' first followers, his disciples. These guys walked with Jesus. They had a front-row seat to Jesus' miracles, conversations, and actions, and they still experienced disappointing faith. Jesus was very aware of this, and how he responded to them is not how I would have responded.

A complicated life is not new. Having a faith that feels disappointing is not new.

Just after watching Jesus heal many people, Matthew wrote in Matthew 8:23-26, "*Then he got into the boat and his disciples followed him. Suddenly a furious storm came up on the lake, so that the waves swept over the boat. But Jesus was sleeping. The disciples went and woke him, saying, 'Lord, save us! We're going to drown!'*

He replied, 'You of little faith, why are you so afraid?' Then he got up and rebuked the winds and the waves, and it was completely calm."

In Matthew 16:8, he wrote, *"Aware of their discussion, Jesus asked, 'You of little faith, why are you talking among yourselves about having no bread?'"*

Luke wrote about a conversation Jesus had with his disciples in Luke 12:22-28: *"Then Jesus said to his disciples: 'Therefore I tell you, do not worry about your life, what you will eat; or about your body, what you will wear. For life is more than food, and the body more than clothes. Consider the ravens: They do not sow or reap, they have no storeroom or barn; yet God feeds them. And how much more valuable you are than birds! Who of you by worrying can add a single hour to your life? Since you cannot do this very little thing, why do you worry about the rest?*

Consider how the wild flowers grow. They do not labor or spin. Yet I tell you, not even Solomon was dressed like one of these in all his splendor. If that is how God clothes the grass of the field, which is here today, and tomorrow is thrown into the fire, how much more will he clothe you - you of little faith!'"

I feel like this is a conversation Jesus could have with me or anyone else who is worried about things they should not worry about. That's not you, of course, but you know people who worry about stuff they should not worry about. A complicated life will do that to people.

Jesus looked straight at the people who followed him the closest and, on more than one occasion, said to them, *"You of little faith."* And every time, he continued to love and accept them. He kept them close, and they continued to follow him.

Peter is one of my favorite guys in the Bible. He, like me, seemed to be an ask-for-forgiveness-later kind of guy who spoke before he thought sometimes. Peter was in the inner circle of Jesus' disciples, yet his faith disappointed him repeatedly.

In Matthew 16:21-23, we read about this interaction between Jesus and Peter: *"From that time on Jesus began to explain to his disciples that he must go to Jerusalem and suffer many things at the hands of the elders, the chief priests and the teachers of the law, and that he must be killed and on the third day be raised to life.*

Peter took him aside and began to rebuke him. 'Never, Lord!' he said. 'This shall never happen to you!'

Jesus turned and said to Peter, 'Get behind me, Satan! You are a stumbling block to me; you do not have in mind the concerns of God, but merely human concerns.'"

Matthew wrote about another conversation between Jesus and Peter in Matthew 14:28-31: *"'Lord, if it's you,' Peter replied, 'tell me to come to you on the water.' 'Come,' he said.*

Then Peter got down out of the boat, walked on the water and came toward Jesus. But when he saw the wind, he was afraid and, beginning to sink, cried out, 'Lord, save me!'

Immediately Jesus reached out his hand and caught him. 'You of little faith,' he said, 'why did you doubt?'"

If I could take Peter to lunch, I'd ask him so many questions. I'd love to walk through Matthew 26:31-75 with him. In these verses, he:

- calls Jesus a liar
- denies knowing Jesus three times
- falls asleep when Jesus specifically asks him to stay awake

- does not stop Jesus from being arrested

Grab your Bible and read these verses. Talk about a complicated, lousy day. Not exactly Peter's faith highlight reel. At the end of that day, verse 75 tells us, "*And he went outside and wept bitterly.*"

Peter "went outside and wept bitterly." Has your faith ever felt so disappointing you wept? Mine has. I remember pulling over on I-85 in Spartanburg, South Carolina because I could not see through my tears. Driving and ugly crying do not go together. I was driving to get medicine for Julie because of the miscarriage and medical procedure she'd just experienced. A miscarriage is terrible for anyone. At that time, we were still walking through infertility. We'd been praying and fasting for this baby. We had a support group of people doing the same for us. That made the miscarriage feel worse than terrible. I don't know the word for how my faith in Jesus felt so disappointing.

Peter experienced a faith in Jesus that felt disappointing. So did the other disciples.

In all these situations, what blows me away is Jesus' response to the disciple's faith. He did not kick them out of his group. He did not stop loving them or accepting them. Yes, he called them out sometimes. Ultimately, he gave them the responsibility of launching his movement to reach the world. That doesn't make sense. Faith doesn't make sense.

WHAT NOW?

It is life-changing and, more importantly, faith-changing to feel the freedom to say to yourself and God your faith in Jesus feels disappointing. Life is too complicated for it not to feel this way sometimes. I've been a pastor for a long time, and I've been me for an even longer time. I know I'm weird, but I think I'm pretty normal, too. I just have this feeling that most Christians are walking through their lives feeling like, "This is it?" when it comes to their faith in Jesus.

I wish we were sitting across the table from each other so I could ask you a question. If we were, I'd ask, "So, when I say it's okay to admit your faith in Jesus is disappointing, how do you immediately respond?" My hunch is your gut reaction would be one of these responses.

I'M AFRAID TO ADMIT THIS ABOUT MY FAITH

Do you live life assuming God will get you at any minute? You may not realize you think this way, but you do. If you do anything wrong, God is going to punish you. You're going to get what you deserve, and you know you deserve bad things.

You're wrong! Sorry to be so blunt. I love you too much to let you think false things like that. God knows all your sins. All of them. Yes, even that one, and He still sent Jesus to die and rise from the dead for you.

If you have started your faith in Jesus, you are forgiven forever. You are loved forever. You are accepted forever. You can admit anything to God; He will forgive, love, and accept you.

I THINK IT'S WRONG TO SAY THIS ABOUT MY FAITH

This line of thinking goes like this: If you admit your faith is disappointing, you are saying God is disappointing. Saying God is disappointing is saying God is bad. If you put God down like that, you are sinning. Sinning is wrong; therefore, admitting your faith is disappointing is a sin.

You're wrong! Sorry to be so blunt. I love you too much to let you think false things like that. Your faith is your faith. How your faith feels says more about you than God or Jesus. They do not change. The prophet spoke for God in Malachi 3:6, *"I the Lord do not change."* And the writer of Hebrews 13:8 wrote, *"Jesus Christ is the same yesterday and today and forever."*

God can not only handle anything you think or say, but He also welcomes your honesty. Even Jesus was brutally vulnerable and honest with God. There is a fantastic scene in Matthew 26 where Jesus goes away to pray alone. He is getting closer to death and understands the suffering he is about to experience. What does Jesus (the Son of God and God in a body) say to God the Father?

In verse 39, he prays, *"My Father, if it is possible, may this cup be taken from me. Yet not as I will, but as you will."*

In verse 42, he prays, *"My Father, if it is not possible for this cup to be taken away unless I drink it, may your will be done."*

And verse 44 tells us he went away and *"prayed the third time, saying the same thing."*

Jesus was 100% honest with God. It is okay to tell God your faith in His Son feels disappointing. Jesus modeled this kind of honesty for us.

THAT'S JUST THE WAY FAITH IS

It concerns me how often we settle for disappointment. We settle for a disappointing marriage, children, physical health, etc. On the one hand, I believe everyone and everything will disappoint you at some time. No one is perfect. You're going to be disappointed. If you know me, I will disappoint you. My favorite restaurant, sports teams, and people disappoint me.

But there is a difference between being disappointed by something and settling for disappointment. When you settle, you are agreeing this is just the way it is going to be. When you believe your faith in Jesus will be disappointing, you're saying, "This is it?" is just how trusting Jesus will be.

You're wrong! Sorry to be so blunt. I love you too much to let you think false things like that. Instead, your faith in Jesus can be "This is it!"

But first...the church. I'm excited about the next chapter, and I'm nervous too. I'm going to try to manage the tension of talking about the one thing Jesus established to reach the world with his message, the thing I've chosen to give my career to, the organization I love the most, and how it has contributed significantly to your feeling like "This is it?" when it comes to your faith.

CONVERSATION QUESTIONS

Do you agree or disagree your faith in Jesus can feel disappointing? Why or why not?

When does your faith in Jesus feel disappointing?

Why does your faith in Jesus feel disappointing? Can you relate to any signs or reasons this chapter listed?

What do you tend to do when your faith in Jesus feels disappointing?

10

THE CHURCH AND YOUR "THIS IS IT?" FAITH

I love the church. Growing up and even after graduating college, I never dreamed I'd be a pastor and church work would be my career. Yet, here I am decades later. I could do something else, but I don't want to.

I have not always loved the church. The church was not where I wanted to be when I was a kid. Maybe, just maybe, when I was a kid, I would sleep on my top bunk every Saturday night in hopes my parents could not reach me when they came to wake me up to go to church on Sunday morning. Maybe I would get in trouble in "big church" laughing at the ladies who sang the "special music" that morning. I promise it sounded more like yelling than singing. I guess they had good hearts because they were not good at singing. They sure did have a lot of confidence. In my defense, my dad laughed too. He never got in trouble for it, though.

Things changed for me in high school and college. The church became a meaningful part of my life. I was fortunate to be around people my age and older who made me feel known and needed.

One year after graduating college and getting married, I quit my good job with a good paycheck and career path and earned my master's degree to become a pastor. I was the last person to know this was what I was supposed to do with my life. Over the years, I have worked at some great churches.

I've had the opportunity to work with churches and church staff in the United States, Canada, Australia, New Zealand, Costa Rica, the Bahamas, the Philippines, the United Arab Emirates, and South Africa. There are many reasons to feel good about the church.

I believe the church was Jesus' idea to reach the world with his good news: there is a way to be right with God and live with Him forever. It cannot lose despite all the internal efforts to screw it up and the external efforts to take it down. It can lose some short-term battles, but the church ultimately wins!

The first time we hear about the church is in Matthew 16:18, when Jesus said to Peter, "*And I tell you that you are Peter, and on this rock I will build my church, and the gates of Hades will not overcome it.*"

Death overcomes everything. Everything dies and goes away, but not the church. Jesus died, and the church went on. Paul died, and the church went on. Wars, evil, heartbreak, etc., happen, and the church continues. You and I will die, and the church will go on. The church cannot be overcome even by death.

In his must-read book *The Grace of God*, Andy Stanley wrote, "Instead of establishing a kingdom, he planted the church. The Greek term translated church simply means 'a gathering.' In this case, it would be a gathering with a very specific purpose. They were to take his message to all nations. Here's Luke's version of a portion of Jesus' final instructions: 'But you will receive power when the Holy Spirit comes on you; and you will be my witnesses in Jerusalem, and in all Judea and Samaria, and to the ends of the earth' (Acts 1:8). This new gathering – later referred to as the church – was established by Jesus as the vehicle for delivering the message of grace to "the end of the earth.'"[24]

The Ross family is very competitive. Our family games can turn into, well, let's just say things have been said and apologies have been made. Just walk by us when we're playing a game on the beach. Actually, don't do that. I want you to think we're good people. We love to win, and we hate to lose. I think it's one of the reasons I love the church so much. It wins in the end!

WHAT IS MORE IMPORTANT THAN HOW

General George Patton was one of the most successful combat generals in U.S. military history. During World War II, he helped free Germany from the Nazis. He was one of the U.S. Army's greatest leaders in any position, and he had some great things to say during his lifetime. Here are just a few of his famous quotes[25]:

- "Lead me, follow me, or get out of my way."
- "If everybody is thinking alike, then somebody isn't thinking."
- "Do everything you ask of those you command."
- "Do more than is required of you."

My favorite Patton quote is this one:

"Never tell people how to do things. Tell them what to do and they will surprise you with their ingenuity."

The church has gotten this wrong, and so have most parents, companies, schools, bosses, etc. But this chapter is about the church. I've worked on different church staffs for decades. I've worked with hundreds of churches and church staff members worldwide. No, I have not worked with every church. I'm sure there are exceptions to what I will say in this chapter, but I can say with confidence most churches get this wrong.

Churches focus more on *how* than *what*. And that contributes to our faith in Jesus feeling disappointing.

Let me get personal before we talk more about the church. In 2019, I was publicly humbled. By whom? I'm glad you asked. It was my "friends" who humbled me. Just when you think you know people, they turn on you. Here is what I posted on Facebook:

"Dear Facebook, please save our marriage! When making a peanut butter and jelly sandwich, what utensil(s) do you use to spread the peanut butter and the jelly?

I know you will be honest and not choose sides, so I'll tell you what is tearing apart our marriage. Julie uses a knife to spread both. I use a spoon to spread the jelly and a knife to spread the peanut butter...like a sane person.

Prove I'm right...I mean, save our marriage."

How would you respond? Yep, I know how you would respond...just like everyone else responded on Facebook. It hurts. I thought we were friends.

Person after person let me know how to make a peanut butter and jelly sandwich. And the correct way is Julie's way. Well, if "correct" is how most people do it. I was honestly surprised. My way made sense to me. Still does.

My wife, and 99% of the world, use one side of a knife to put the peanut butter on the bread and the other side of the same knife to put the jelly on the bread. Over and over, I was laughed at, questioned, and made fun of for how I make a PB&J.

I still believe the best way to make a PB&J is the way I do it. Julie is rolling her eyes and saying, "Of course you do." The narrow knife is perfectly made to collect and spread the peanut butter. The wider spoon is perfectly made to collect and spread the jelly. This makes sense, right? I've convinced you to do it my way, right? I know. You're not changing anything.

When I was a kid, I was told *what* to do...make a peanut butter and jelly sandwich. And I did it. No one told me how to do it. They just told me *what* to do. So, I came up with my way to do it, and in the end, I eat a delicious PB&J just like you.

Please don't tell Julie about what I'm about to tell you.

I have a hard time letting other people drive. If someone other than Julie drives, I can keep my words, facial expressions, and gestures about his or her driving to myself. It isn't easy. When Julie drives, though, it all comes out. I try hard to keep it all in, but I fail. Julie is a great driver. She's never had a wreck that was her fault except when she hit that mailbox. She's never gotten a ticket. No one ever honks at her. She always gets to her destination...eventually. But *how* she drives is very different from *how* I drive.

I love driving. I consider myself a good driver. I may drive a little aggressively sometimes, but I am safe about it. You can drive aggressively and safely, right?

Think about driving. The *what* is always the same: Get to your destination. But the *hows* are so numerous:

- How far in advance will you turn on your turn signal?
- When will you change lanes?
- How fast will you drive?

- When will you use cruise control?
- When will you brake?
- Which roads will you take to your destination?
- How much distance will you put between you and the vehicle in front of you?
- How low will you let the gas get?
- Should you honk or flash your lights at another driver when they bother you?
- When will you use your windshield wipers? I think we almost went to marriage counseling over this *how*.
- How loud will the music be?
- When will you merge into the other lane when your lane is ending?
- Should you let the other car go ahead of you?
- Who goes next at the four-way stop?
- How fast will you drive through a curve?
- Is the sunroof open or closed?
- How far back will you put your seat?
- How cold will you set your AC?

We get so obsessed with *how* people do things. It's not just me. You do it too. There is a right and wrong way to do "it." And "it" is just about anything and everything. The right way is almost always the way you do it.

Julie has an odd *how*. She doesn't think it's weird, but I do. She has a very specific *how* when wiping down our kitchen countertops. I've attempted to be a good husband several times and wipe down the countertops. I don't do that anymore. I did it wrong; I'm not sure how I did it wrong, but I did. Julie had to wipe them down to fix how I wiped them down.

Have you ever noticed there is usually more than one way to do something? We determine the "right" way based on what we value, our past, and many other factors we're usually unaware of. We see our way as the right way when it's just our preferred way.

We're not talking about PB&Js, traffic, and countertops anymore.

Churches spend most of their time and energy on *how*. They tell people *how* to do faith. *How* to grow it, live it, share it, etc. There is a method, book, plan, and formula for every part of your faith.

You follow the *hows* or the formula your church gives you until they bore or disappoint you. Then you find a new church with a "better" *how* or formula.

Patton said, "Never tell people how to do things. Tell them what to do and they will surprise you with their ingenuity." I wish the church adapted a version of his quote. Maybe "Never tell people *how* to have a better faith. Tell them to trust Jesus more and they will surprise you with their ingenuity." Many of us aren't sure how to practice ingenuity with our faith in Jesus. I hope the rest of this book changes that.

YOUR FAITH IS NOT LIKE A MATH PROBLEM

I'm not good at math. I do not know how I passed high school or college math classes. No, I didn't cheat. (That was high school chemistry class...sorry, Mom.) All three of my kids are good at math. Thanks to Julie, they're good at most subjects. They stopped asking me for help with math homework in early elementary school, and I completely understood.

The math I hated the most in school involved formulas. I just did not get formulas. You know, something like:

$a + y^2 - x + b / 7 + tree - lamp = blue$

Ugh. I can't even make up a math formula.

I've noticed people with faith in Jesus treat their faith like a formula. Me included. It makes you feel confident. It makes you feel like you are close to God. It makes your complicated life and faith feel manageable. See if any of these feel familiar:

- give money + volunteer + be in a small group + invite people to church = faith
- be held accountable + read many books + attend small group = faith
- attend Sunday School + attend weeknight outreach = faith
- give money + give more money = faith
- confess sins to a spiritual leader + memorize lots of spiritual words = faith
- raise your hands when singing + sway back and forth while singing + pump your fists while singing = faith
- wake up early to pray + journal your prayers + have coffee with a Christian = faith
- feel guilty about sins + feel shame about your past + go to church = faith

Almost all churches would tell you faith is not a formula. Of course, it's not, but they do not lead you this way. Churches treat your faith like a math problem because formulas create predictability.

Churches prefer predictability because it helps them plan, hire, budget, attract people, promise results, and differentiate themselves from other churches. You prefer predictability because it helps you achieve your goal of having both feet on the ground. You feel safe when you feel in control or at least able to manage life.

However, predictability does not require faith. Do you need to trust Jesus when everything is predictable? No. Instead, you trust the formula that creates predictability. The more you follow the formula, the more faith you have. That's what you think, but that's not trust. That's safe activity, which leaves you bored and disappointed.

Predictability is a good thing in math. It is a hallucination in life and faith. Our complicated life does not allow life to be predictable. That is why faith in Jesus is so important. Faith in anything or anyone else will let you down. Faith in a formula will eventually let you down. Faith in Jesus is the solution.

When the church treats your faith like a math problem to be solved, you inevitably ask, "This is it?" regarding your faith in Jesus.

THE CHURCH FOCUSES ON HOW

Most churches care a lot about *what* they want for you. They want your faith in Jesus to grow. They pray for your faith to grow, but they don't practically focus on that. They hire, budget, promote, measure results, etc., based on the *hows* they offer. The church's resources (time, people, money) are spent more on *how* than *what*. See if any of these *hows* sound familiar:

- small groups
- church membership
- financial giving
- confession
- volunteering
- confirmation classes
- mission trips
- memorized prayers
- baptism
- church retreats

- Sunday school
- accountability groups
- nights of worship
- prayer meetings
- communion
- women's ministries
- vacation Bible school
- revival services
- infant baptism
- outreach night
- Bible studies
- community groups
- first communion
- membership classes
- men's ministries
- mentoring
- catechism classes

You get the point. Every one of these things is *how* a church says you can achieve a better faith. These are the things the church emphasizes, and these are the things you focus on when it comes to your faith in Jesus. Instead of increasing your actual trust in Jesus, you spend your time being busy doing the *hows* your church promotes.

You do what your church tells you to do and eventually you find yourself wondering, "This is it?"

All of the *hows* are meaningful. They are important to me, you, the church, and others, but they are not the most important thing. The *hows* make a dangerous assumption.

ONE SIZE DOES NOT FIT ALL

My three kids have the same dad and the same mom. I'm sure of that. I was in the room when all three were born. They've grown up in the same house, gone to the same schools, eaten dinners around the same table, been supported by the same fantastic mom, and had to listen to the same bad dad jokes. They even look alike. And my three kids could not be more different from each other.

They eat different foods, have different personalities, relate to others differently, communicate differently, recharge differently, feel loved differently, show love differently, learn differently, and on and on and on.

What if Julie and I parented them the same? It would make our lives easier. We could manage our family more efficiently. We'd be less tired, but that would not be the best thing for our kids. We'd end up with less meaningful relationships with each one of them. They would not feel known by us. We'd end up less connected to them, and they'd probably end up needing counseling one day. Who am I kidding? They're going to need counseling one day. I'm their dad.

We're all different. Yes, we have significant things in common, yet you're different from me. Stop and thank the Lord for that. Each one of us has:

- a one-of-a-kind story
- a different family of origin
- different learning styles
- a unique perspective
- personal preferences
- different learning challenges

When a church emphasizes *how*, they are assuming one size fits all. If any person would just do what they say to do, their faith would grow. It just does not work that way.

Think about what led you to start your faith in Jesus. Was it God's kindness, His conviction, a significant life event, a dream, a meaningful relationship, a logical argument, an encounter with a stranger, the presentation of specific information, or something else?

What leads each of us to start a faith in Jesus is different for each of us. What helps us grow our faith in Jesus is different for each of us. That is why *what* is more important than *how*.

THE CHURCH IS TRYING ITS BEST

I love the church, but I believe it's gotten some things wrong about faith (not intentionally, of course.) I've been a part of the church getting it wrong.

I hope this does not come as a surprise: People lead the church - normal people. (Well, some are less normal than others.) People tend to do one thing with anything they get their hands on: They try to manage it. They want to control it so they can measure it and make it do what they want. That's human nature. That's not always a bad thing.

The church is no different. The church, led by people, tries to manage faith by focusing on *how* instead of *what*. The church attempts to manage faith so it can measure faith and make it do what they think faith should do. It's all with good intentions, and a lot of good things happen because of this. Most churches are simply trying their best. No church is perfect.

Christians have some interesting expectations of church. When I say "interesting," I mean weird, sad, ridiculous, funny, confusing, and selfish expectations. Some of the more common and less weird expectations I've heard are more Christian knowledge, more Christian friendships, more Christian feelings, more Christian events, and more Christian activities.

I guess you want more because your natural drift is toward complexity. Life never naturally drifts you toward easy and less. It drifts you toward more and more complicated. You cannot help this drift. You can only choose to fight against it.

And the church tries to keep up with your expectations. Y'all, it is not easy. The church is just trying its best to help you.

So, the church keeps writing prescriptions for you.

- Do this two times each month for six months...
- Do this one time each week for 18 months...
- Stop doing this and do this daily...
- Do this every morning forever...

...and you will find what you're looking for from the church and God. It may work for a little while, but it eventually stops working. And we wonder, "This is it?" concerning our faith in Jesus.

What if your church decided not to focus on telling you *how* to have better faith? What if the church told you to trust Jesus more, and you surprised them with your creative ways to trust Jesus more?

YOUR FAITH IS LIKE A RELATIONSHIP

Before we end this chapter, let's circle back to something we discussed a few pages ago. Your faith in Jesus is not like a math formula. Thank You, God! So, what is your faith like then? Our attempts to put words to God and faith all fall short. So, let's try to put some words around what your faith in Jesus is like.

Faith in Jesus is like a relationship.

I don't know about you, but every meaningful relationship I have is messy and beautiful. A meaningful relationship takes risks and trust.

Treat your faith in Jesus like a relationship, not a math formula. Faith is not a subject to be learned or an assignment to be turned in. It is not a task to complete or an activity to sign up for. Your faith in Jesus is like a relationship, and relationships grow as trust increases.

Pastor Ian Simkins said, "A truth that haunts me is that it's entirely possible to spend one's life devoted to the mission of Jesus as a substitute for being devoted to the person of Jesus. Doing things for God is not the same thing as doing things with God. Activity is a terrible trade-off for intimacy."[26]

Intimacy is a characteristic of any real, meaningful relationship. Intimacy is created over time through trust. Your faith in Jesus is like a relationship. It's messy; it's not black and white. There's intimacy built through increasing trust, not through one-size-fits-all activities.

What can you do to increase your trust in Jesus? I am so glad you asked. You're going to love the next chapter.

WHAT NOW?

The church was Jesus' idea and plan to reach the world. Make yourself known and needed in your church. Don't wait for the church to look for you. Approach your church like Jesus. In Philippians 2:3-7, Paul wrote this about him, *"Do nothing out of selfish ambition or vain conceit. Rather, in humility value others above yourselves, not looking to your own interests but each of you to the interests of the others.*

In your relationships with one another, have the same mindset as Christ Jesus:

Who, being in very nature God, did not consider equality with God something to be used to his own advantage; rather, he made himself nothing by taking the very nature of a servant, being made in human likeness."

I'm a pastor, so I want to speak on behalf of churches. I don't know a pastor who is completely satisfied with the "results" he or she sees in their church. Results can be serving, financial giving, small group attendance, worship attendance, and many other things. But the result I hear pastors most disappointed in is the absence of people in the church experiencing and living out in the community a faith in Jesus that yells, "This is it!"

"Your system is perfectly designed to get the results you're getting." I've heard Andy Stanley say something like that so many times. Your system is *how* you do things and accomplish things. Your system is the *hows* you emphasize. So, if a church is not ultimately happy with the results it sees in its people who have put their faith in Jesus, the *hows* must change.

Check out "Appendix 2: For Church Leaders" for some specific steps the church can take to help people grow their faith and rely less on church for their faith.

If you're asking, "This is it?" when it comes to your faith in Jesus, you must change *how* you do your faith. How you are living out your faith is resulting in a "This is it?" faith. Your faith is your responsibility. Get creative in how you trust Jesus more.

We need a new way of seeing and experiencing how we do our faith in Jesus. The next chapter is going to be fun!

CONVERSATION QUESTIONS

How do you make a peanut butter and jelly sandwich?

When do you trust a formula that creates predictability instead of trusting Jesus more? Can you write out the formula?

What church "*hows*" do you currently rely on for better faith?

How do you rely on your church or someone else to grow your faith in Jesus?

How is your faith in Jesus like a relationship?

11

FAITH IS STEPS (AND IT TAKES ONE STEP)

What is your greatest fear?

I have to share my answer with you because I would never ask you something I'm unwilling to answer. I'll tell you about one of my greatest fears.

I have a fear of heights. I'm afraid of heights because I don't want to fall from way up there. If I fall from high up, it will not end well. I prefer not to have broken bones or be dead. I consider what I would think as I fall from way up there. The higher the height, the more time I'd have to think about falling as I fall. No, thank you!

Atlanta has a great sports and concert venue called Mercedes Benz Stadium. It looks like a spaceship on the outside. For the record, I don't have any experience seeing a real spaceship, so I may be wrong. When it was being built, I knew the guy in charge of all the steel being used in the construction. I was not too shy to leverage that relationship so I could check out the stadium during construction.

On one occasion, my friend asked if I wanted to go to the top of the stadium. He mentioned the only way to get up there was to climb temporary stairs from the third level to the top of the stadium. He warned me it could be frightening for people afraid of heights or not used to climbing this type of step. I am a man with a fragile ego, so, of course, I said, "I'm not afraid." I even kind of laughed arrogantly to show my confidence. I lied. His brief description of the climb made me terrified and sweaty.

When we got to the stairs, I thought about faking the flu, diarrhea, hallucinations, blindness, anything that would get me out of it. Are you familiar with a scaffold stair tower? They are temporary stairs assembled in the middle of scaffolding that sway and bounce with each step you take. Oh yeah, and wobbly handrails that shake with each step. Plus, no walls, so you can see 360 degrees around you. And you can see between every step and through the holes on every step and landing.

Don't worry, though. I was required to wear a bright orange safety vest and a hard hat. That way, you could easily see my body falling through the air when I fell to my death. I'm pretty sure there was no way the helmet would stay on my head long enough to pretend to protect me when I hit the ground.

I death-gripped the handrails with both hands for 12 flights of stairs and the wood ramp up the side of the stadium roof. I thought about each step I took up the stairs and then up the ramp onto the top of the roof. I made it to the top! The view of Atlanta was awesome, as was seeing the construction of the retractable roof. So worth the near-death experience.

Then I had to go back down. That was way worse. I'm not kidding.

I believe fear is the most influential emotion you feel. Fear causes you to say and do so many things. It causes you to:

- say the right thing

- say the wrong thing
- not say the right thing
- not say the wrong thing
- do the right thing.
- do the wrong thin
- not do the right thing
- not do the wrong thing

Sound familiar?

Yes, other emotions influence you. I hope love greatly influences your words and actions, but fear is powerful. Pastors, politicians, marketers, teachers, and parents use fear to get their audiences to do what they want; it often works.

Fear is why you seek shallow water. Fear is why you pray for both feet to be firmly planted on the ground. Fear is why you've tricked yourself into thinking easy and peaceful is what God wants for you. You fear the deep end where your feet don't touch the bottom. You're afraid because your complicated life has taught you to fear what could be next.

WHERE DOES YOUR COURAGE COME FROM?

Your best response to fear is courage. That's not a big surprise. Where do you find courage in your life? Do you just decide to have courage? No. Do you find it deep within yourself? No. You must take action to receive the courage to overcome your fear.

Trust is your source of courage. You overcome your fear when you trust someone or something. Julie and I dated for six years before we got married. Okay, not exactly six years. I mentioned our two "unfortunate separations" in college when I was an idiot. No need to go into the details again. Outside those two situations, we had a smooth, fun, and pretty easy relationship. So, when we decided to get married, it felt like the natural next step in our relationship. No big deal, right?

Wrong! Marriage is a ginormous decision. I don't care how great of a relationship you have; there is fear in the decision to commit to a relationship with the same person for the rest of your life. Especially when one of them broke up with the other one two years in a row on her birthday. When you marry someone, you choose to trust that person. Your trust in that person gives you the courage to overcome, or at least outweigh, any fear you have about marrying them.

No matter what or who you choose to trust, you trust them for a desired outcome. You want something from them. This kind of trust will always let you down. It's inevitable. You can't stop that thing or that person from disappointing you.

When you trust Jesus, you find the courage you need for this complicated life. When you take a step to trust Jesus more, He proves trustworthy. He gives you the courage to take the next step, the next step, and so on. You find the courage to overcome your fear when you trust Jesus.

John 16 lets us in on a conversation between Jesus and his disciples. It wasn't what his disciples expected to hear or wanted to hear. Jesus was going to leave them soon because he would die soon. And here is what confused them. In verse 7, he said, *"But very truly I tell you, it is for your good that I am going away. Unless I go away, the Advocate will not come to you; but if I go, I will send him to you."* The Holy Spirit would only come after Jesus was gone. And it was far better for them to each receive the Holy Spirit than to have Jesus walking around with them.

In verse 33, Jesus said something to them that he is saying to us today, *"I have told you these things, so that in me you may have peace. In this world you will have trouble. But take heart! I have overcome the world."* This world will be complicated. It will be difficult. You will feel fear. But you can trust Jesus! You will find peace when you trust Him. He has overcome the world. He won! Starting your faith in Jesus is truly the only way to have the courage to overcome your fears.

WHEN LIFE FORCES YOU INTO THE DEEP END

Life is complicated on our best days. On other days, life can be cruel. As I write this, we know people dealing with situations like:

- terminal illness
- a child with a learning disability
- looking for a new job
- mysterious illness
- childhood cancer
- surgery
- aging parents
- divorce
- the death of a child
- abuse
- addiction
- identity theft
- mental illness
- debt

Life just seems to punish you at times. And there is nothing you can do about it.

How does life feel in these moments? It feels deep. It feels like your feet cannot touch the bottom. When your feet reach for the bottom, nothing is there. You're in the deep end. You feel out of control, in danger, and helpless. You feel fear.

Not being able to touch the bottom and trust go together. If you feel like your feet are planted on the bottom, you do not have to trust Jesus. You may have trusted Him at some point, but you do not have to trust Him now. That's not faith.

Matthew told a story about Jesus in Matthew 8:5-10. He wrote, *"When Jesus had entered Capernaum, a centurion came to him, asking for help. 'Lord,' he said, 'my servant lies at home paralyzed, suffering terribly.'*

Jesus said to him, 'Shall I come and heal him?'

The centurion replied, 'Lord, I do not deserve to have you come under my roof. But just say the word, and my servant will be healed. For I myself am a man under authority, with soldiers under me. I tell this one, 'Go,' and he goes; and that one, 'Come,' and he comes. I say to my servant, 'Do this,' and he does it.'

When Jesus heard this, he was amazed and said to those following him, 'Truly I tell you, I have not found anyone in Israel with such great faith.'"

The centurion was in the deep end. His servant was "suffering terribly." I don't think we need to know the details to know it was bad. This person was obviously suffering. You've probably been in a situation where someone you cared about was "suffering terribly." You felt helpless, like you could not touch the bottom.

The centurion had such deep faith that Jesus was "amazed." Jesus was not amazed by his knowledge, words, or prayers. He was amazed by his trust. Someone the centurion cared about was suffering. The centurion was suffering, watching the servant suffer. At that moment, the centurion could not touch the bottom. All he knew to do was to trust Jesus at that moment, and Jesus was amazed at this faith.

Even people with no faith often think about God when they cannot touch the bottom. Something about those moments causes a person's thoughts and emotions to drift toward God, even if there is anger toward God or questioning directed at God.

What should you do when life forces you into the deep end?

First, trust Jesus. Let him know you trust him. That may be all you can do. The centurion trusted Jesus. He had a very specific outcome he desired. He wanted his servant to be healed. He let Jesus know this, but he trusted Jesus more than he desired the outcome.

Next, lean into your church for support. Make your church aware of how you're in the deep end and how you need help. I hope you are a part of a church that cares about individuals and families in the deep end. These are beautiful churches. I'm not saying the church should meet all your needs or do precisely what you want them to do, but I do hope they make you feel loved and cared for.

Finally, lean into others to support you. Let others know how you're in the deep end and how you need support. "Others" could be friends, doctors, local support organizations, counselors, etc. Your faith in Jesus does not exclude you from help from others.

It's interesting. When life pushes you into the deep end, your trust in Jesus often grows. It happens because it's like you have nowhere else to turn. You don't know what else to do. So, you trust Jesus with your situation. You tell him that. You trust him when your feet cannot touch the bottom.

WHEN LIFE FEELS GOOD

Most of life is good, or at least it feels okay. It's still complicated, but it's good. These are the days you pray for. This is your goal in life. You're in the shallow end with both feet feel planted on the ground.

It's often in these times, however, when your faith in Jesus feels most like, "This is it?" You try to fix that disappointed feeling with all the *hows* the church promotes and the faith formulas you think will fix your faith. Yet, you end up knowing something is missing from your faith.

How do you grow your faith in Jesus when life feels good?

How do you trust Jesus more and more in the shallow end?

How can your faith in Jesus feel like "This is it!" when life is just normal?

I'm glad you asked.

You need to answer these questions if you're going to have faith that feels like "This is it!" If you have started your faith in Jesus, the Spirit of God lives inside of you. Your life, with God in you, cannot look the same as everyone else. There is no condemnation for you. You are forgiven. You have eternal hope. Faith in Jesus should affect everything about you and around you. Let's have this kind of faith in Jesus. How? Here we go!

FAITH IS STEPS

We defined a step as a decision to say something or do something. Steps may not seem significant, but each step matters. Steps, even good steps, scare you. Each step forces you to ask, "What's next?" and "What if...?"

We discussed how the church says you can grow your faith in Jesus, but you and I are unique. What causes you to trust Jesus more differs from what causes me to trust Jesus more. Focusing on the *hows* and formulas only leads to "This is it?" faith.

So, what do you do to grow your faith in Jesus? Can you really trust Jesus, without the *hows* and formulas, more and more when life is okay? Yes! **"This is it!" faith happens when you understand faith is steps and take steps that cause you to trust Jesus more.** What do these steps look like?

STEPS THAT CAUSE YOU TO NEED JESUS TO SHOW UP

To live well in this complicated life, you need to take steps. The critical distinction between those steps is the direction of the steps. Keep moving forward, not backward or standing still.

Steps that cause you to trust Jesus are forward steps, but they are also steps that cause you to pause, feel nervous, and need Jesus' help. They don't have to be big, significant steps. They can be small steps, but they are steps that make you whisper, "Jesus, I need you to help me with this."

When you take this kind of step, you feel something on the other side of the step. On the other side, you whisper, "Thank you, Jesus!"

Rachel Held Evans and Jeff Chu wrote, "At its best, faith teaches us to live without certainty and to hope without guarantee. At its best, faith teaches us to take risks."[27]

Mark Sayers says, "Yet as we will find in the economy of God, challenge carries a different value. It becomes a precious resource. The presence of God transforms challenge into spiritual growth.

Yet many can miss out on the spiritual growth that occurs in times of challenge. When something is challenging or difficult, we often retreat. Our culture has created the idea of comfort zones, the idea we can be both successful while avoiding discomfort. However, this myth prevents us from growing and moving into renewal."[28]

Risk. Challenge. Difficult. Uncomfortable. These are the kinds of steps that will grow your faith and cause you to feel like, "This is it!"

REGULARLY TAKE STEPS

I think we intuitively know faith is steps. You've experienced it when life forced you into the deep end, and the only thing you thought to do was trust Jesus. You've taken a step that made you need Jesus to show up, and He proved trustworthy. So why do you rely on the church's *hows* or formulas to grow your faith?

You see steps as something to do only on an as-needed basis. You only take steps that cause you to trust Jesus when you have to. Steps are for the big things in life: job change, marriage, medical decisions, etc. You don't make steps a regular part of your life and faith.

To have a "This is it!" faith in Jesus, you must regularly take steps that cause you to trust Jesus. Daily. Weekly. In seemingly insignificant times. The goal is to develop a habit of taking steps that cause you to trust Jesus more. Habits are formed by repeating the same action until you do it without realizing it. Can you imagine if taking steps to trust Jesus more became a habit in your life? "This is it!"

To get there, regularly take steps. You'll be very aware of each step at first. That's okay. Take a step. Take another step. Then another step. Look for opportunities to use your words and actions in ways you need Jesus to show up so you can say or do the right thing.

TAKE UNIQUE NEXT STEPS

I love the phrase "unique next steps" when it comes to taking steps to grow your faith in Jesus. The steps that will cause me to trust Jesus more are different from those that will cause you to trust Jesus more. Take steps that cause you (not your kids, parents, friends, etc.) to trust Jesus more.

Our daughter Bennett was in a sorority when she was in college. She even became the Vice President. Then at the end of one school year, she let us know she was dropping out of the sorority. She felt like it was a step she needed to take; a step that caused her to have to trust Jesus more. She had invested a lot of relationships, time, energy, and money into this group.

Would this have been a step that caused me to have to trust Jesus more? No. I'm not a big fan of these kinds of groups, so it would have been easy for me to drop out. Would this have been a step that caused her friends to have to trust Jesus more? For some, yes. For some, no. None of that matters. This was a unique next step for Bennett because it caused *her* faith in Jesus to grow.

HAVE A DEEP FAITH

The word "deep" is such a rich word. Think about it:

- deep friendship
- deep passion
- deep knowledge
- deep relationships
- deep conversations

"Deep" implies intimacy and meaningfulness only experienced with a few people or topics. How can you experience a deep faith in Jesus? Remember, our faith is like an intimate relationship.

Deep faith is experienced through trusting Jesus more and more. Bible study, quiet times, worship, etc. can help you have a deep faith when you use those things to help you take a step that causes you to trust Jesus more.

If you have not started your faith in Jesus and life puts you in a situation where you cannot touch the bottom, lean into your thoughts and feelings toward God. Go deep.

If you feel far from God, take a step where you cannot touch the bottom. Go deep.

If you feel something is missing in your faith, take a step where you cannot touch the bottom. Go deep.

If you feel your church is not providing something for your faith, take a step where you cannot touch the bottom. Go deep.

I want to help you take steps that cause you to trust Jesus more. Your steps will be different from other people's steps. I want the word "deep" to stick in your mind and heart regarding steps. I want your steps to put you in the deep end where you cannot touch the bottom, and you trust Jesus more.

If you're unsure what a unique next step could be for you, let's get practical.

EXAMPLES OF UNIQUE NEXT STEPS

- start your faith in Jesus
- become friends with a neighbor
- work fewer hours
- ask for help
- coach your kid's team
- see a counselor
- attempt to repair a damaged relationship
- make your spouse feel loved
- share that thing you're afraid to share
- give money to the person holding the sign that says they need help
- get baptized
- make peace with someone
- start a new job
- see a doctor about your health concerns
- mentor kids in a local school
- defend someone who needs defending
- help someone having car trouble
- give financially to your church
- join the board of a local nonprofit
- get help concerning the dangerous habit you have
- make your kids feel loved
- read the Bible daily
- make the other person feel loved in every interaction
- be kind to someone you don't like
- increase your financial giving to your church

These are unique next steps. I don't know what word or action would cause you to have to trust Jesus more, but you know. What feels like a risk or makes you nervous? What needs to be said or done, but you're putting it off because you feel fear? Your trusting Jesus with this step will give you the courage to take the step.

If you'd like to see more examples of unique next steps, check out "Appendix 1: More Unique Next Steps" at the end of the book.

IT ONLY TAKES ONE STEP

One step is all it takes. I'm serious. Just one. What is the one step that will change your faith in Jesus? It's your next step.

So much is riding on your decision to take or not take that one step. What could happen if you take it? At the very least, your faith in Jesus could grow. That's life-changing. That one step is one step away from a faith that feels disappointing.

Who knows how else you and others could benefit from you taking this one step to trust Jesus more? Remember Romans 8:28? Paul wrote, *"And we know that in all things God works for the good of those who love him, who have been called according to his purpose."* Who knows what good God will do when you take this one step?

What if you don't take this one step? How will this affect you and those around you?

You can do it! Take one step. Yes, it will take courage to take the step. Jesus will prove trustworthy when you trust him to help you take the step. When you experience this, it will make it a little bit easier to take the next step. When you take the next step and the next step, you create the habit of growing your faith or trust in Jesus.

WHAT NOW?

As much as I want you to keep reading, the point of this book is to help you have a "This is it!" faith in Jesus. Please take a day or week off reading and take one step that causes you to trust Jesus more. Take a unique next step that causes you not to be able to touch the bottom. I want that for you. I have prayed for you to get in the habit of taking these kinds of steps. Then come back and finish reading the book. I think the final three chapters will help you even more.

Let your church love you if you're in a season when life is cruel, and you've been forced into the deep end. Let the people around you love you and help you. You may have to take a step to trust Jesus by sharing your news and your needs, but you can do it.

CONVERSATION QUESTIONS

What are your greatest fears?

When has life forced you into the deep end where you could not touch the bottom? Did your trust in Jesus increase during this time?

What step will you take that will cause you to trust Jesus more?

How can you create a habit of taking steps that cause you to have to trust Jesus more?

12

FAITH CELEBRATED IN THE BIBLE

Every morning when cute, little first-grade students walk into Julie's classroom, they start on green/ "ready to learn." Throughout the day, if they make good choices, Julie tells them to move their clip up to blue/"outstanding" and then purple/"extraordinary." But, if they make poor choices, she tells them to move their clip down to orange/"make better choices" and then red/"talk about a consequence."

If a student ends the day in blue or purple, they get rewarded. Her students almost always end the day in green, blue, or purple. Why?

"What's rewarded gets repeated."[29]

This can happen negatively also. Allow me to be your example for this.

Our family loves to laugh, and we like to make each other laugh. Sometimes we say things about someone else in our family, and it gets a laugh. Don't worry; it's lighthearted and safe. When one of our kids says something about Julie (aka their mom and my wife), and I laugh, my laughter is perceived as a reward. When I celebrate them with my laughter, they'll probably say something again about her to try to get another laugh out of me.

It's all fun and games until they go too far. Then one day, they're getting in trouble for something I've been celebrating. Oops. My bad. Stay tuned for my parenting book coming out soon.

What kind of faith does God celebrate? What kind of faith gets celebrated in the Bible? Have you ever paid attention to that? If you knew the answers to those questions, would it make you want to repeat the kind of faith that gets celebrated? There could be a lot to learn in answering those questions.

HEBREWS 11

You'd have my attention if your name were mentioned in the Bible, along with a comment about something you did because you trusted God. I'd even take notes. Hebrews 11 lists names and what people did to get their names mentioned in the Bible. So, I'm paying attention.

Hebrews 11 starts with this in verse one, "*Now faith is confidence in what we hope for and assurance about what we do not see. This is what the ancients were commended for.*"

Who are "the ancients?" Hebrews 11 mentions Abel, Noah, Abraham, Sarah, Moses' parents, Rahab (a prostitute), Gideon, and other names. It also mentions "the prophets" and "others." And there is story after story of the words and actions these people displayed as they trusted God.

Hebrews 11 ends in verse 39, "*These were all commended for their faith.*" There is no mention of them being celebrated for their knowledge or worship. They were celebrated for their trust that showed up in their words and actions.

One phrase is mentioned over and over throughout Hebrews 11: "by faith."

"By faith…" these people trusted God with their words and actions. They took unique next steps in a complicated life that caused them to trust God more. And God noticed and proved trustworthy.

What "by faith…" steps have you taken in the past when life was cruel?

What "by faith…" steps have you taken in the past when life was good?

What is your next "by faith…" step?

THE CENTURION

I've mentioned him before, but it's worth mentioning again the guy whom Jesus said this about: *"I have not found anyone in Israel with such great faith."* Matthew even wrote that Jesus was amazed by his faith. I want to know about this guy's faith. What gets celebrated gets replicated.

Life was cruel to someone the centurion cared about. He hurt because someone he loved was hurting. He felt like he could not touch the bottom. He wanted peace and control, and he could not find it. So, he turned to Jesus. I've felt like this before. Can you relate?

Matthew wrote in chapter 8:5-13, *"When Jesus had entered Capernaum, a centurion came to him, asking for help. 'Lord,' he said, 'my servant lies at home paralyzed, suffering terribly.'*

Jesus said to him, 'Shall I come and heal him?'

The centurion replied, 'Lord, I do not deserve to have you come under my roof. But just say the word, and my servant will be healed. For I myself am a man under authority, with soldiers under me. I tell this one, 'Go,' and he goes; and that one, 'Come,' and he comes. I say to my servant, 'Do this,' and he does it.'

When Jesus heard this, he was amazed and said to those following him, 'Truly I tell you, I have not found anyone in Israel with such great faith. I say to you that many will come from the east and the west, and will take their places at the feast with Abraham, Isaac and Jacob in the kingdom of heaven. But the subjects of the kingdom will be thrown outside, into the darkness, where there will be weeping and gnashing of teeth.'

Then Jesus said to the centurion, 'Go! Let it be done just as you believed it would.' And his servant was healed at that moment."

When I read about this situation, I want to find a formula. If I do this and say this and believe this, then Jesus will fix the hurt and pain I am experiencing. Maybe you can relate?

I remember trying formulas when we were going through infertility and when I was leading a struggling church about to close. I was open to trying anything to make the pain and difficult decisions disappear. Yet, all along, God was most interested in my faith.

When looking for a formula, I focus on the *how*, not the *what*. The centurion did not say the magic words. He did not even ask Jesus what he could or should do to make the bad disappear. He had faith in Jesus. That's it. There is no code to unlock here. There is a person to trust. A formula does not require trust.

ABRAM

In Genesis 15:1-6, we read, *"After this, the word of the Lord came to Abram in a vision:*

'Do not be afraid, Abram. I am your shield, your very great reward.'

But Abram said, 'Sovereign Lord, what can you give me since I remain childless and the one who will inherit my estate is Eliezer of Damascus?' And Abram said, 'You have given me no children; so a servant in my household will be my heir.'

Then the word of the Lord came to him: 'This man will not be your heir, but a son who is your own flesh and blood will be your heir.' He took him outside and said, 'Look up at the sky and count the stars - if indeed you can count them.' Then he said to him, 'So shall your offspring be.'

Abram believed the Lord, and he credited it to him as righteousness."

Andy Stanley, in his best book (just my opinion) *The Grace of God*, wrote, "As Abram stared at the black canopy of space littered with billions of stars, he made a critical choice. He decided to believe God. Despite the lack of tangible evidence and in spite of his working knowledge of human reproduction and the effects of age on procreation, Abram placed his trust in God's character. He believed in the Lord's integrity to follow through on his promises; Abram trusted God's power to accomplish the impossible.

And then something remarkable happened.

In response to Abram's faith, God declared him righteous. God said, in effect, because you have trusted in me, I give you the gift of righteousness. I have written forgiven across your moral ledger sheet. Because of your faith, I have cleared your account of all debt. At that very moment, the Lord established an important precedent: a righteous standing with God comes through faith. This is the single most important aspect of God's grace."[30]

From the beginning, God has cared the most about the *what*. Trust Him.

MOSES

Where do we even start with Moses? He trusted God over and over by taking step after step. Just follow his story:

- He returned to Egypt to free his people from Pharaoh.
- He confronted Pharoah to his face.
- He led the people out of Egypt.
- He parted the Red Sea as the enemy pursued them.
- He met with God on Mt Sinai to receive God's rules for His people.
- He led the people in the wilderness for 40 years.

We think of Moses as this superhero-like person from the Bible. I believe Moses thought of himself as an ordinary man who wanted to do what God wanted him to do. In Exodus 4:10-13, we read, *"Moses said to the Lord, 'Pardon your servant, Lord. I have never been eloquent, neither in the past nor since you have spoken to your servant. I am slow of speech and tongue.'*

The Lord said to him, 'Who gave human beings their mouths? Who makes them deaf or mute? Who gives them sight or makes them blind? Is it not I, the Lord? Now go; I will help you speak and will teach you what to say.'

But Moses said, 'Pardon your servant, Lord. Please send someone else.'"

This conversation happened in the middle of God giving Moses his mission and his authority. Before any of the events happened that made him famous, Moses felt ordinary. He felt inadequate. Can you relate? I can.

Over and over, life had Moses in situations where he felt fear. Over and over, his life was complicated (and that's putting it mildly), but he found the courage to take steps forward by trusting God. He took steps that caused him to have to trust God repeatedly.

JESUS' MOM AND DAD

We know it all worked out just fine. Better than fine. Their son became the Savior of the world. But Joseph and Mary had no idea how it would turn out. All they knew was a very complicated beginning.

In Matthew 1:18-21 and 24, we read about when Joseph's life got really complicated really quickly. *"This is how the birth of Jesus the Messiah came about: His mother Mary was pledged to be married to Joseph, but before they came together, she was found to be pregnant through the Holy Spirit. Because Joseph her husband was faithful to the law, and yet did not want to expose her to public disgrace, he had in mind to divorce her quietly.*

But after he had considered this, an angel of the Lord appeared to him in a dream and said, 'Joseph son of David, do not be afraid to take Mary home as your wife, because what is conceived in her is from the Holy Spirit. She will give birth to a son, and you are to give him the name Jesus, because he will save his people from their sins.'

When Joseph woke up, he did what the angel of the Lord had commanded him and took Mary home as his wife."

In Luke 1:28-38, we read about when Mary's life got really complicated really quickly. *"The angel went to her and said, 'Greetings, you who are highly favored! The Lord is with you.'*

Mary was greatly troubled at his words and wondered what kind of greeting this might be. But the angel said to her, 'Do not be afraid, Mary; you have found favor with God. You will conceive and give birth to a son, and you are to call him Jesus. He will be great and will be called the Son of the Most High. The Lord God will give him the throne of his father David, and he will reign over Jacob's descendants forever; his kingdom will never end.'

'How will this be,' Mary asked the angel, 'since I am a virgin?'

The angel answered, 'The Holy Spirit will come on you, and the power of the Most High will overshadow you. So the holy one to be born will be called the Son of God. Even Elizabeth your relative is going to have a child in her old age, and she who was said to be unable to conceive is in her sixth month. For no word from God will ever fail."

'I am the Lord's servant,' Mary answered. 'May your word to me be fulfilled.' Then the angel left her."

Life was normal and good. Mary and Joseph were going to get married. Then life got complicated. Surprise! Mary was pregnant, and it was not Joseph's baby. Then life got even more complicated. Joseph was going to do the right thing and quietly end their relationship. Then life got really complicated. On separate occasions, an angel told them her baby was from God.

How would you have responded? No, seriously, how would you have responded? I would have freaked out like a professional freaker-outer.

Joseph *"did what the angel of the Lord had commanded him and took Mary home as his wife."*

Mary told the angel, "*I am the Lord's servant. May your word to me be fulfilled.'* *Then the angel left her."*

Remarkable trust. Not trust in themselves. Not trust in each other. Trust in God.

ANANIAS

Ananias is on your Fantasy Faith Team, right? He's not on mine, either. Honestly, he was not on my original list of people from the Bible to discuss in this chapter. Then I read Acts 9. His faith does not clearly get rewarded, but he is mentioned as a main character at the beginning of Paul's faith story.

In Acts 9:1-19, we read, *"Meanwhile, Saul was still breathing out murderous threats against the Lord's disciples. He went to the high priest and asked him for letters to the synagogues in Damascus, so that if he found any there who belonged to the Way, whether men or women, he might take them as prisoners to Jerusalem. As he neared Damascus on his journey, suddenly a light from heaven flashed around him. He fell to the ground and heard a voice say to him, 'Saul, Saul, why do you persecute me?'*

'Who are you, Lord?' Saul asked.

'I am Jesus, whom you are persecuting,' he replied. 'Now get up and go into the city, and you will be told what you must do.'

The men traveling with Saul stood there speechless; they heard the sound but did not see anyone. Saul got up from the ground, but when he opened his eyes he could see nothing. So they led him by the hand into Damascus. For three days he was blind, and did not eat or drink anything.

In Damascus there was a disciple named Ananias. The Lord called to him in a vision, 'Ananias!'

'Yes, Lord,' he answered.

The Lord told him, 'Go to the house of Judas on Straight Street and ask for a man from Tarsus named Saul, for he is praying. In a vision he has seen a man named Ananias come and place his hands on him to restore his sight.'

'Lord,' Ananias answered, 'I have heard many reports about this man and all the harm he has done to your holy people in Jerusalem. And he has come here with authority from the chief priests to arrest all who call on your name.'

But the Lord said to Ananias, 'Go! This man is my chosen instrument to proclaim my name to the Gentiles and their kings and to the people of Israel. I will show him how much he must suffer for my name.'

Then Ananias went to the house and entered it. Placing his hands on Saul, he said, 'Brother Saul, the Lord - Jesus, who appeared to you on the road as you were coming here - has sent me so that you may see again and be filled with the Holy Spirit.' Immediately, something like scales fell from Saul's eyes, and he could see again. He got up and was baptized, and after taking some food, he regained his strength."

Let me translate Ananias' reply to Jesus when he told him to go to Saul. This is a very loose, not-even-close translation. "Umm, Lord. It sounds like you said to go to Saul. Isn't that funny? I must have heard you wrong. My bad. Saul is the last person you'd send me to. He can arrest me and throw me in jail, and he's also really good at killing people just for following you. Say that one more time, please."

Ananias walked the steps to the home where Saul was staying. And he took the figurative steps to approach Saul, put his hands on him, and tell him the message Jesus gave him. Because he took steps to trust Jesus more, Saul was given his mission. Saul would be renamed Paul and become one of the most influential Jesus followers ever.

THE WOMAN WITH THE BLEEDING PROBLEM

In Mark 5:25-34, we read about a woman who had suffered physically, and no doubt emotionally, for 12 years. *"And a woman was there who had been subject to bleeding for twelve years. She had suffered a great deal under the care of many doctors and had spent all she had, yet instead of getting better she grew worse. When she heard about Jesus, she came up behind him in the crowd and touched his cloak, because she thought, 'If I just touch his clothes, I will be healed.' Immediately her bleeding stopped and she felt in her body that she was freed from her suffering.*

At once Jesus realized that power had gone out from him. He turned around in the crowd and asked, 'Who touched my clothes?'

'You see the people crowding against you,' his disciples answered, 'and yet you can ask, 'Who touched me?''

But Jesus kept looking around to see who had done it. Then the woman, knowing what had happened to her, came and fell at his feet and, trembling with fear, told him the whole truth. He said to her, 'Daughter, your faith has healed you. Go in peace and be freed from your suffering.'"

Like you and me, the woman did everything she could to fix her medical problem. I remember the second time we went through IVF to try to get pregnant. We saw great doctors and nurses and went into a lot of financial debt. Julie did not get pregnant. We would have done anything to have a baby, just like this woman would have done anything to stop her bleeding.

In her desperation, she took a step to trust Jesus. It doesn't sound like she was that familiar with him. She'd only heard about him, but she felt hopeless, and her only chance at hope was Jesus. Jesus called her "daughter" and rewarded her faith in him. The intimacy of that name. The miracle of that moment.

I don't know why her faith healed her medical issue and why my faith did not heal our medical issue. Trust isn't in the outcome. Trust is in the person of Jesus.

THE CRIMINAL ON THE CROSS

Okay, this one can bother some people. I get that. However, we must get comfortable with it because Jesus was comfortable with it. In Luke 23:32-43, we read, *"Two other men, both criminals, were also led out with him to be executed. When they came to the place called the Skull, they crucified him there, along with the criminals - one on his right, the other on his left. Jesus said, 'Father, forgive them, for they do not know what they are doing.' And they divided up his clothes by casting lots.*

The people stood watching, and the rulers even sneered at him. They said, 'He saved others; let him save himself if he is God's Messiah, the Chosen One.'

The soldiers also came up and mocked him. They offered him wine vinegar and said, 'If you are the king of the Jews, save yourself.'

There was a written notice above him, which read: THIS IS THE KING OF THE JEWS.

One of the criminals who hung there hurled insults at him: 'Aren't you the Messiah? Save yourself and us!'

But the other criminal rebuked him. 'Don't you fear God,' he said, 'since you are under the same sentence? We are punished justly, for we are getting what our deeds deserve. But this man has done nothing wrong.'

Then he said, 'Jesus, remember me when you come into your kingdom.'

Jesus answered him, 'Truly I tell you, today you will be with me in paradise.'"

Jesus is dying on the cross. He's being made fun of. Two other guys, both legit criminals, are also dying on crosses. One of the criminals joins in with the others and makes fun of Jesus. The other criminal responds differently. He simply requests that Jesus remember him when he enters heaven, and Jesus answers by granting his request.

This is faith? A simple request? What did the criminal have to lose? Nothing. You've been in this kind of situation before. You were not facing a death sentence, of course, but you had nowhere else to turn. You were in the deep end and could not touch the bottom, and your last ounce of energy was about to run out. You asked Jesus for help. Last-minute faith is faith, too.

WHAT NOW?

"What's rewarded gets repeated."

The faith celebrated in the Bible has nothing to do with knowledge. It has nothing to do with a formula. It has nothing to do with activity or correct beliefs.

The faith that is talked about in the Bible has everything to do with words and actions. An active trust in God and His Son Jesus is what is celebrated and rewarded.

Matthew told a parable about trusting Jesus. In typical parable fashion, he used a scenario and objects the people listening would understand. In Matthew 25:14-30, he wrote, "*Again, it will be like a man going on a journey, who called his servants and entrusted his wealth to them. To one he gave five bags of gold, to another two bags, and to another one bag, each according to his ability. Then he went on his journey. The man who had received five bags of gold went at once and put his money to work and gained five bags more. So also, the one with two bags of gold gained two more. But the man who had received one bag went off, dug a hole in the ground and hid his master's money.*

'*After a long time the master of those servants returned and settled accounts with them. The man who had received five bags of gold brought the other five. 'Master,' he said, 'you entrusted me with five bags of gold. See, I have gained five more.'*

'*His master replied, 'Well done, good and faithful servant! You have been faithful with a few things; I will put you in charge of many things. Come and share your master's happiness!'*

'*The man with two bags of gold also came. 'Master,' he said, 'you entrusted me with two bags of gold; see, I have gained two more.'*

'*His master replied, 'Well done, good and faithful servant! You have been faithful with a few things; I will put you in charge of many things. Come and share your master's happiness!'*

'*Then the man who had received one bag of gold came. 'Master,' he said, 'I knew that you are a hard man, harvesting where you have not sown and gathering where you have not scattered seed. So I was afraid and went out and hid your gold in the ground. See, here is what belongs to you.'*

'His master replied, 'You wicked, lazy servant! So you knew that I harvest where I have not sown and gather where I have not scattered seed? Well then, you should have put my money on deposit with the bankers, so that when I returned I would have received it back with interest.

"So take the bag of gold from him and give it to the one who has ten bags. For whoever has will be given more, and they will have an abundance. Whoever does not have, even what they have will be taken from them. And throw that worthless servant outside, into the darkness, where there will be weeping and gnashing of teeth.'"

The master tells the two servants who did something with their money, "Well done, good and faithful servant." I don't know how you will be rewarded for your faith in Jesus while you are alive or when you're in heaven. It does not matter. What matters is you trust Jesus. I wonder when you take a step that causes you to trust Jesus more if Jesus thinks these words about you: "Well done, good and faithful servant."

CONVERSATION QUESTIONS

What stands out to you about the faith celebrated in the Bible?

Who in the Bible stands out to you because of their faith?

Whom do you personally know whose faith in Jesus stands out to you?

What would it feel like for Jesus to look at you and say, "Well done, good and faithful servant."?

What "by faith..." steps have you taken in the past when life was cruel?

What "by faith..." steps have you taken in the past when life was good?

What is your next "by faith..." step?

13

EVERYBODY'S WATCHING

Will all the people watchers please raise their hand? It's okay. This is a safe place.

I see that hand, and I'm giving you a high-five. I love people watching. I love to observe people's behaviors and interactions. People are so cool and funny and weird to me. I don't do it to make fun of anyone. I do it because people fascinate me. I can only imagine the awkward comedy I provide for people watching me.

I am very aware there is a fine line between people watching and being creepy. On more than one occasion, my kids have pointed out they think I have crossed that line, but I think I'm skilled at people watching.

Where are the best places to people watch? Here's my list, in no particular order:

- the airport
- the beach
- church
- restaurants

- anywhere you can buy things
- stuck in traffic
- the pool
- my house

Okay, that makes it sound like I people watch everywhere. I do. If people are around, I'm watching.

Let's be honest. Even you non-people watchers watch people. Everybody is watching everybody else. No one is flying under the radar. And that's not a bad thing for us Jesus-followers.

YOUR SUPERPOWER

If you could have one superpower, what would it be?

My wife has had the same answer to this question since we met in high school. She would want her superpower to be flying. She has dreams about being able to fly. I think there is some psychological classification for people who dream about flying, but I don't judge.

What would I want my superpower to be? That is a tough question for me to answer. I over analyze all the superpowers, their pros and cons, and how I could use them for good and evil. I mean how I could use them for good and better. Yeah, that's it.

For me, it comes down to two superpowers: super speed and flying. Super speed would be awesome. I could get everywhere I wanted to go so fast. No traffic. You wouldn't even see me go past you. I'd be where I am, and then I'd be where I want to be. That would be nice, but I have to go with flying. I love flying in general and the view it gives you. I would love the ability to fly over traffic and get places faster. I'd love just to be able to fly around whenever I want. And bonus! Julie and I could fly around together. How sweet.

I believe you have a true superpower, and you use it every day for good and evil. Well, maybe evil is too extreme. You use it for good and not-so-good all the time. I believe it is the most powerful thing about you.

What is your superpower? Influence.

"Influence" means "the power or capacity of causing an effect in indirect or intangible ways."[31]

Your words and actions affect people you know and people you don't know. People you're aware of and people you are not aware of. You influence everyone around you throughout your day. When you:

- like someone's social media post, you influence how they feel about themselves.
- don't go when the light turns green because you're distracted by your phone; you influence everyone behind you.
- buy a shirt at the store; you influence the people looking for the same shirt after you.
- say kind words to the person checking you out at the grocery store; you influence how they treat other customers.
- don't tell someone how much they mean to you; you influence your relationship with them.
- let someone go ahead of you in traffic; you influence their schedule.

You make a difference in people's lives all day, every day. How does that make you feel? Powerful? Responsible? Fearful?

166

I have proven I am not perfect. And you're humble enough to admit you're not perfect. So, we must accept our influence is not always positive. You affect people in negative ways. I assume you're an awesome person, but you still affect people in negative ways. Sometimes you influence people in negative ways on purpose. That's just wrong. As your friend, I'm just going to say it: Stop that.

More often, you influence people in negative ways without knowing you did it. This is the scary part of influence. You're constantly influencing people, but you're not constantly aware of your influence.

UNINTENTIONAL INFLUENCE

Have you ever been driving a car and suddenly realized you don't remember the last few minutes of driving? You're still going in the right direction. You're safe. You kind of laugh about it, but it also kind of scares you.

That's what unintentional influence is like.

We go through our day. We get done all we need to get done. Nothing bad happened. We ended the day satisfied with what we did and who we were with. There is a long list of people we influenced, and we were unaware of them or our influence on them.

Unfortunately, we often do not pay attention to our influence. Why does this matter so much? There is too much at stake in our everyday lives to not care about our influence.

This is a problem to solve. There is another way, a better way, to influence people. You can use your superpower to be a hero in people's lives.

INTENTIONAL INFLUENCE

I wasn't the worst big brother ever, but I wasn't exactly the best either. There was the time I hit the record button on my boombox in my room and then walked down to Mike's room. Yes, one of those large, rectangular silver stereos. I taunted him like a pro, then ran back to my room...where the boombox was recording whatever sounds it heard. Of course, he followed me back to my room to let me have it, just like I had planned. I recorded everything he said, and he said some impressively mean things to me. I took my evidence to my parents to get him in trouble, and nothing happened. Apparently, I was not as bright as I thought. It was apparent to everyone that I was evil and set him up.

That is a fantastically evil example of intentional influence. I could not have been more intentional about my influence on him. The problem was me. Let's just hope I've matured since then.

When you intentionally influence someone, you pay attention to how you affect them. You are thinking about the results your words and actions will have on them.

What should a Christian's intentional influence look like?

The writer of Hebrews in Hebrews 10:24 wrote, *"And let us consider how we may spur one another on toward love and good deeds...."*

You should consider how every word you say and every action you do may influence someone toward love and good deeds. If your goal is to help others experience and show love and motivate them to do good things for others, there are words you won't say and actions you won't do. And there are words you will say and actions you will do. That is how a Jesus-follower practices intentional influence.

Matthew wrote in Matthew 5:14-16, *"You are the light of the world. A town built on a hill cannot be hidden. Neither do people light a lamp and put it under a bowl. Instead they put it on its stand, and it gives light to everyone in the house. In the same way, let your light shine before others, that they may see your good deeds and glorify your Father in heaven."*

You are supposed to act like light. Light is only useful when turned on so people can see better. A Christian's light is our words and actions. Your words and actions should shine like a light on a stand. The purpose of the light is to help others. Did your words and actions today shine like a light that helped others and put attention on God in a positive way? When you are intentional with your influence, you do things that help others and put positive attention on God.

How intentional are you with your influence? To be intentional with your influence, you may need to take a step that causes you to trust Jesus more. Intentional influence is not always easy.

The influence of someone who has faith in Jesus can change a life, a family, a community, and a world. That's you and me. Our world is too complicated, and people are hurting too much for us to be unintentional with our influence. I believe people are looking at you and me. They are watching us to see if faith in Jesus matters. A "This is it?" faith tells them faith in Jesus does not matter.

Will people see a "This is it?" faith or a "This is it!" faith when they watch you?

EVERYONE IS WATCHING YOU IN A NON-CREEPY WAY

You're being watched. And that's something you should get excited about.

Your faith in Jesus should cause you to speak and live so differently that you live better in this complicated life than someone who has not started their faith in Jesus. If you have started your faith in Jesus and no one knows or notices a big difference, that is a problem. Did you really put your faith in Jesus? I don't know. That is between you and Jesus.

No, you do not need to live perfectly. I am not encouraging you to be some religious weirdo. (Please don't be that Christian.) I'm saying, please talk and act like someone who obviously trusts Jesus in a complicated world. When bad things happen, and you cannot touch the bottom, trust Jesus. And, when life is good, take steps to trust Jesus more. Let people see your faith in Jesus is the most important thing about you.

You know some of the people watching you, and you'd be surprised to learn some of the people watching you. It's safe to assume everyone is or will be watching you. And that is good news!

Some people are watching you because they know you have faith in Jesus. Some people are watching because you're close by and will take notice when your trust in Jesus is obvious. It's safe to assume everyone is or will be watching you. That's good news!

In Matthew 14:22-33, Matthew wrote, "*Immediately Jesus made the disciples get into the boat and go on ahead of him to the other side, while he dismissed the crowd. After he had dismissed them, he went up on a mountainside by himself to pray. Later that night, he was there alone, and the boat was already a considerable distance from land, buffeted by the waves because the wind was against it.*

Shortly before dawn Jesus went out to them, walking on the lake. When the disciples saw him walking on the lake, they were terrified. 'It's a ghost,' they said, and cried out in fear.

But Jesus immediately said to them: 'Take courage! It is I. Don't be afraid.'

'Lord, if it's you,' Peter replied, 'tell me to come to you on the water.'

'Come,' he said.

Then Peter got down out of the boat, walked on the water and came toward Jesus. But when he saw the wind, he was afraid and, beginning to sink, cried out, 'Lord, save me!'

Immediately Jesus reached out his hand and caught him. 'You of little faith,' he said, 'why did you doubt?'

And when they climbed into the boat, the wind died down. Then those who were in the boat worshiped him, saying, 'Truly you are the Son of God.'"

There are so many things that stand out in this interaction between Jesus and his disciples. My favorite thing about this interaction is the disciples. Peter was being watched. They watched Peter walk on water. They watched Peter sink into the water. They heard the conversation between Peter and Jesus. They watched the wind die down, and they took it all in. Every word and action of Peter influenced them.

Yet Peter was not doing this because he was being watched. He was simply taking steps that caused him to trust Jesus more. Nonetheless, people were watching.

At the end of this interaction, the disciples' response is fantastic. *"Truly you are the Son of God."* They understood Jesus was the Son of God after they saw

Peter trust Jesus. Wait! They were Jesus' disciples. They'd left all they had to follow him. They'd seen him do incredible things. They'd heard him say and teach great things, and watching Peter trust Jesus more is when they finally got it. Jesus was the Son of God.

The writer of Psalm 40, in verses 1-3, wrote,
"I waited patiently for the Lord;
he turned to me and heard my cry.
He lifted me out of the slimy pit,
out of the mud and mire;
he set my feet on a rock
and gave me a firm place to stand.
He put a new song in my mouth,
a hymn of praise to our God.
Many will see and fear the Lord
and put their trust in him."

Many people will see the Lord through the writer's words and actions. And they will start their faith.

People are watching you. Take steps to trust Jesus more. The faith of others is at stake.

GIVE THE PEOPLE WHAT THEY WANT

I genuinely believe the people around you want to see your faith in Jesus lived out in a way that proves it makes you better at life. People are desperate for hope, and most of us have figured out money, success, politics, and relationships do not provide long-term hope. Only Jesus provides that kind of hope, yet very few Christians live out a "This is it!" faith, so very few non-Christians believe the hope-filled claims of Jesus.

In his book *Not In It To Win It*, Andy Stanley wrote, "Believing has become a substitute for following. We've been so focused on not substituting works for faith that many of us have quit working. Or in Paul's words, we quit working out our faith.

Authentic faith does stuff."[32]

Paul wrote in Ephesians 2:8-10, *"For it is by grace you have been saved, through faith – and this is not from yourselves, it is the gift of God – not by works, so that no one can boast. For we are God's handiwork, created in Christ Jesus to do good works, which God prepared in advance for us to do."* Yes, your faith is only possible because of God's grace. He gives you something you do not deserve. You cannot earn or deserve your faith in Jesus. But...

Once you start your faith, you should get to work doing *"good works."*

Don't fall for the lie that believing the right things about Jesus is what matters the most. It does not. The world, yes, the whole world, needs to see you and me doing good works and working out our faith in Jesus. There is too much at stake for you to keep living like believing matters more than doing.

Live out your growing faith in Jesus in front of everyone by taking steps that cause you to have to trust Jesus more.

WHAT NOW?

If you have a job, your coworkers, customers, and boss watch you.

If you are a student, your classmates and teachers watch you.

If you're a parent, your kid watches you.

If you have a significant other, your better half watches you.

If you live near other people, your neighbors watch you.

If you play sports, your teammates, opponents, and coaches watch you.

If you're in a club, the other members watch you.

If you cheer for your favorite team, your team's fans and the other team's fans watch you.

If you're in a family, your family members watch you.

If you're a human, everyone around you watches you every day.

What do they see? Do they see a person who talks and acts pretty much like they talk and act? Do they see a person who reacts to the cruel parts of life as they react? Do they see a person who makes decisions like they make decisions? Those are the signs of a "This is it?" faith. And no one is looking for that kind of faith.

Do they see a nice person who goes to church? Do they see someone who just does less bad stuff than they do? Do they see someone whose goal is to make life easy? Do they see a person who is usually kind to strangers? Those could be the signs of a "This is it!" faith. Or those could be the signs of a nice person who goes to church. That's boring.

Do they see someone who talks and acts very differently than they do? Not in a judgmental way. Not in an I'm-better-than-you way - in a way full of love for all people; a way that makes everyone and everything around them better; in a way that shows trust in Jesus. Those are the signs of a "This is it!" faith. People are searching for this even if they do not realize it.

Show the world around you what it is like to trust Jesus in a complicated world. Have a "This is it!" faith that makes you come alive and positively affects everyone around you.

CONVERSATION QUESTIONS

If you could have one superpower, what would it be?

How much influence do you think you have? Why did you answer that way?

What will you do to improve your intentional influence?

What, in general, do you think people see when they watch you?

What kind of faith in Jesus do people see when they watch you?

14

THIS IS IT! (WHEN LIFE AND FAITH FEEL MEANINGFUL)

I have a confession to make. You've made it this far. I should come clean.

I've had an agenda the whole time you've been reading. Yes, I want you to take steps that cause you to trust Jesus more. I hope that's been clear.

But I've also had a hidden agenda. Here it is. Don't be mad. I want you and I to own our faith in Jesus.

I have pastor friends who laugh at me when I tell them this is what I want for you. They want this for you, too, but they say you won't do it. They say the church has trained you not to own your faith in Jesus. They say we humans are too focused on ourselves to truly have a "This is it!" faith we own.

Let's show my pastor friends, the church, and, most importantly, the world what it looks like for people who have faith in Jesus to own their faith by taking steps to trust Jesus daily. It'll change you and change the world. Isn't that why Jesus came?

Let's stop relying on all the things we rely on for our faith:

- the church
- a pastor or priest
- sermons
- curriculums
- your spouse
- your parents
- your kids
- some other person
- the country you live in
- all the *hows* the church promotes
- events
- the times in life when we're forced into the deep end
- made up faith formulas
- _____ (insert what / who you rely on)

I want you to stop studying faith like it's science class. Remember your high school science class? You read, listened to lectures, took notes, and studied to learn information. Then you applied the knowledge you learned in some lab experiment or on a test. Lab days were always my favorite days. Then you moved on to the next topic in the textbook and repeated the process all over again.

I want you to take forward steps in life. I want you to take steps that cause you to trust Jesus more often. Yes, in the big things, but especially in the small things. It's in the common areas of life where our lives go from "This is it?" to "This is it!"

YOUR FAITH IS UP TO YOU

We love to start things. We don't exactly love to keep up with the things we start. Okay, we usually stink at it. Not you, of course. You follow through like a champ. Know anyone, though, who has started a gym membership, book, diet, goal, workout program, etc. lately? I bet they started strong. How are they doing now?

We have a similar relationship with our faith in Jesus. Starting your faith in Jesus is 100% a personal decision. It's totally up to you if and when you make that decision. No one can decide for you or even tell you when to make it. Starting your faith in Jesus is your responsibility, and you start strong.

Then something happens. Things change. Life gets more complicated. Then you act like it is the church's or someone else's responsibility to grow your faith in Jesus. Why?

A. You view starting faith as the finish line instead of the starting line.
B. You are fearful and want someone to tell you what to do.
C. You think growing your faith in Jesus means memorizing information and feeling something.
D. You try to grow your faith but feel like, "This is it?"
E. You attend all the gender, age, and season-of-life church events and get addicted to the event experience.
F. You are lazy and want someone else to tell you what to do.
G. All of the above.

In school, I always felt like multiple-choice questions were trick questions. I could overanalyze a multiple-choice question like a pro. That might explain my extremely average grades. Before you laugh at me, Cs get degrees. No tricks here, though. Can I humbly answer "G" for all of us? For decades, I've watched myself and so many other Christians do "A" through "F" over and over. They all result in "This is it?" faith in Jesus.

When you do not own your faith in Jesus, you will move from church to church, curriculum to curriculum, event to event, preacher to preacher, and *how* to *how*. Sound familiar? It does to me. I've seen it hundreds of times. We've got to stop this. People are watching, and it hurts our faith in Jesus.

If you choose to own your faith in Jesus, you can have a "This is it!" faith. Take forward steps to live well in this complicated life. Take steps that cause you to trust Jesus more. Make your faith your faith. James agrees.

JAMES

James is one of my favorite people in the Bible. Talk about a complicated life. He had a brother named Jesus. Yes, that Jesus. That may sound awesome, but it complicated things. Most people did not accept Jesus. James and the rest of the family did not accept Jesus. In Mark 3:21, we read, "*When his family heard about this, they went to take charge of him, for they said, 'He is out of his mind.'*" And in John 7:5, we read, "*For even his own brothers did not believe in him.*" Life was complicated just because life has always been complicated, but when your brother says he is God's Son and the Savior of the world, your life gets extra complicated.

Then we read in 1 Corinthians 15:4-7 where Paul wrote this about Jesus, "*that he was buried, that he was raised on the third day according to the Scriptures, and that he appeared to Cephas, and then to the Twelve. After that, he appeared to more than five hundred of the brothers and sisters at the same time, most of whom are still living, though some have fallen asleep. Then he appeared to James, then to all the apostles,*"

James knew his brother had died. Then James saw his dead brother was not dead. Jesus was alive. That might be the only way I'd believe my brother was the Son of God and the Savior of the world too. James did not believe

Jesus was who he said he was until after his death and resurrection. And it changed his life. We read in Galatians 1:19, Galatians 2:9, Acts 12:17, and Acts 15:13-21 James became a visible and vocal leader of his brother's movement and church.

The brother of Jesus went from rejecting his brother's claims to putting his faith in his brother. And he took forward steps and steps that caused him to have to trust his brother so often he became a leader in his brother's church. We have numerous examples of times he was present in critical moments in the church. And we have a letter he wrote to fellow believers in his brother. What did James think was important?

In James 1:2-4, he wrote, *"Consider it pure joy, my brothers and sisters, whenever you face trials of many kinds, because you know that the testing of your faith produces perseverance. Let perseverance finish its work so that you may be mature and complete, not lacking anything."*

When life is complicated, you can take steps to move forward in life. Not if you face trials, but when you face trials. You can take steps that cause you to trust Jesus more. See the complications in life as opportunities for your trust in Jesus to increase.

In James 1:22-25, he wrote, *"Do not merely listen to the word, and so deceive yourselves. Do what it says. Anyone who listens to the word but does not do what it says is like someone who looks at his face in a mirror and, after looking at himself, goes away and immediately forgets what he looks like. But whoever looks intently into the perfect law that gives freedom, and continues in it - not forgetting what they have heard, but doing it - they will be blessed in what they do."*

Listening, learning, and studying the Bible are all good, but just listening, learning, and studying the Bible is not enough. If you only do these things, you're misleading yourself. You're not doing faith right.

To get faith right, we must apply the Bible, live it, do it, and be consistent. Applying the Bible in ways that cause you to trust Jesus more leads to a "This is it!" faith.

In James 2:14-26, he wrote, *"What good is it, my brothers and sisters, if someone claims to have faith but has no deeds? Can such faith save them? Suppose a brother or a sister is without clothes and daily food. If one of you says to them, 'Go in peace; keep warm and well fed,' but does nothing about their physical needs, what good is it? In the same way, faith by itself, if it is not accompanied by action, is dead.*

But someone will say, 'You have faith; I have deeds.'

Show me your faith without deeds, and I will show you my faith by my deeds. You believe that there is one God. Good! Even the demons believe that – and shudder.

You foolish person, do you want evidence that faith without deeds is useless? Was not our father Abraham considered righteous for what he did when he offered his son Isaac on the altar? You see that his faith and his actions were working together, and his faith was made complete by what he did. And the scripture was fulfilled that says, 'Abraham believed God, and it was credited to him as righteousness,' and he was called God's friend. You see that a person is considered righteous by what they do and not by faith alone.

In the same way, was not even Rahab the prostitute considered righteous for what she did when she gave lodging to the spies and sent them off in a different direction? As the body without the spirit is dead, so faith without deeds is dead."

Okay, James. You are getting rather aggressive now, aren't you? But if you've read this far, his words sound familiar. He's talking about a "This is it!" faith.

If your faith does not include doing the right thing, your faith is dead. What is the right thing to do? Love. Your faith is your faith, but the purpose of your faith is other people. Your faith helps you live better in this complicated life, but your faith, when lived out, benefits others. Faith in Jesus is not faith if you're not saying and doing things that cause you to trust Jesus more and show love to people more.

Moving from a "This is it?" life and faith is not difficult. It takes one step. It involves change, and we fear what we will lose when confronted with change. What will you lose? You will lose that "This is it?" feeling of disappointment you've gotten so used to.

After all, we've talked about, it comes down to one question that will be your catalyst for a thriving life and faith. Ready? Here is the question:

WHAT IS YOUR UNIQUE NEXT STEP?

Your next step in life and faith will be unique to you. This is *your* life and *your* faith in Jesus. It's not your pastor's, spouse's, kid's, parent's, small group leader's, etc. next step. It is your next step.

Whether life is cruel and painful or pretty peaceful right now, what forward step will you take to say and do the right thing?

Whether life is cruel and painful or pretty peaceful right now, what step will you take that will cause you to trust Jesus more?

My insecurities come out a little bit right now. What is a forward step or a step of trusting Jesus for me may be no big deal for you. What if my unique next steps don't impress you? What if you think there is no way my unique next steps could possibly cause me to trust Jesus more? Thankfully, I'm off the hook, and so are you.

For times like this, Paul wrote in Romans 14:5-13, *"One person considers one day more sacred than another; another considers every day alike. Each of them should be fully convinced in their own mind. Whoever regards one day as special does so to the Lord. Whoever eats meat does so to the Lord, for they give thanks to God; and whoever abstains does so to the Lord and gives thanks to God. For none of us lives for ourselves alone, and none of us dies for ourselves alone. If we live, we live for the Lord; and if we die, we die for the Lord. So, whether we live or die, we belong to the Lord. For this very reason, Christ died and returned to life so that he might be the Lord of both the dead and the living.*

You, then, why do you judge your brother or sister? Or why do you treat them with contempt? For we will all stand before God's judgment seat. It is written:

'As surely as I live,' says the Lord, 'every knee will bow before me; every tongue will acknowledge God.'

So then, each of us will give an account of ourselves to God.

Therefore let us stop passing judgment on one another. Instead, make up your mind not to put any stumbling block or obstacle in the way of a brother or sister."

The whole point of my steps is my trust in Jesus increases. If your faith is more mature and more active than my faith, awesome! I'm just trying to catch up and keep up. Don't look down on me. Cheer me on in a way that lets me know you're there for me. Your encouragement will only help me take more steps.

As you take your next steps in life and faith, life will remain complicated. Good and bad will continue to run on parallel tracks. Good people will continue to suffer while bad people continue to prosper. Relationships will continue to be beautiful and messy at the same time.

Instead of feeling disappointed about life and faith, what Jesus said in Luke

6:47-49 can be true of your life and faith in him. *"As for everyone who comes to me and hears my words and puts them into practice, I will show you what they are like. They are like a man building a house, who dug down deep and laid the foundation on rock. When a flood came, the torrent struck that house but could not shake it, because it was well built. But the one who hears my words and does not put them into practice is like a man who built a house on the ground without a foundation. The moment the torrent struck that house, it collapsed and its destruction was complete."*

Forward steps and taking steps to trust Jesus more are like digging down below the surface and laying the foundation of your life on rock. There will be times when life is cruel, and you cannot touch the bottom. When your foundation is rock, you can manage these times with your faith in Jesus and the support of those around you. There will be times when you can touch the bottom. Now, you know to take steps in those times that make it feel like you're not touching the bottom. Your foundation on rock allows you to take steps that feel risky that cause you to trust Jesus more.

ARE YOU REALLY GROWING YOUR FAITH IN JESUS?

Are you trusting Jesus more? Is your faith in Jesus growing? Do you feel qualified to gauge your faith? Can others help you know how you're living out your faith? Can you know the answers to these questions?

If you want to take this seriously, I've got something you can try. Visit caseyross.net and check out the free resources in the "Your Faith & Resources" section. One of the free resources you can use is "Personal Faith Assessment." It's a resource that will help you answer the question, "Am I really growing my faith in Jesus?" It's all about your fruit!

Matthew recorded these words of Jesus in Matthew 7:16-20, *"By their fruit you will recognize them. Do people pick grapes from thornbushes, or figs from thistles? Likewise, every good tree bears good fruit, but a bad tree bears bad fruit. A good tree cannot bear bad fruit, and a bad tree cannot bear good fruit. Every tree that does not bear good fruit is cut down and thrown into the fire. Thus, by their fruit you will recognize them."*

Yes, you can gauge your faith in Jesus. You can tell if your faith is growing. You can ask others to measure your faith objectively. Just look at your fruit. What words and actions are you producing? What are the results of your life on the people around you?

What fruit should you be looking for?

Paul wrote in Galatians 5:22-25, *"But the fruit of the Spirit is love, joy, peace, forbearance, kindness, goodness, faithfulness, gentleness and self-control. Against such things there is no law. Those who belong to Christ Jesus have crucified the flesh with its passions and desires. Since we live by the Spirit, let us keep in step with the Spirit."*

Remember, when you start your faith in Jesus, the Holy Spirit is deposited into you. His presence in you produces specific actions in and through you. And when you take steps in life and your faith in Jesus, these actions show up even more:

- love
- joy
- peace
- forbearance (patience)
- kindness
- goodness
- faithfulness
- gentleness

- self-control

If you are growing in your faith in Jesus, these nine things will show up more and more in your words and actions. You should notice this happening through you, and those around you should experience them from you.

When you take steps that cause you to feel like you cannot touch the bottom in life, you trust Jesus more. As you take these steps, your faith in Jesus becomes more mature and active. A growing faith will also produce fruit in your life...the fruit the Holy Spirit produces in someone with increasing faith in Jesus.

A "This is it!" life and faith are possible. You can tell if you're living it. Don't measure your faith by your feelings or knowledge. Measure your life and faith by your fruit. That's what Jesus said to do.

WHAT NOW?

This is our last "What Now?" section, and this one is easy.

What now? **Ask yourself: What is my unique next step?**

Where do you need to take a step forward in life? What step do you need to take that will cause you to trust Jesus more?

Take that step. It just takes one step.

Then ask yourself: What is my unique next step?

Take that step. It just takes one step.

Then ask yourself: What is my unique next step?

Take that step. It just takes one step.

Then ask yourself: What is my unique next step?

In 2 Corinthians 5:7 (Christian Standard Bible), Paul wrote, *"For we walk by faith, not by sight."*

Start walking by faith. Don't worry about what you cannot see. Faith is trust. Trusting Jesus more and more is what leads you to a "This is it!" life and faith in Jesus.

CONVERSATION QUESTIONS

Do you genuinely own your faith in Jesus?

How do you hold the church, other people, events, etc., responsible for your faith in Jesus?

What would James say about your faith in Jesus?

What unique next step will you take that will cause you to trust Jesus more?

Which of the nine things listed in Galatians 5 needs to be more evident in your words and actions? What steps will you take to make this happen?

Appendix 1: More Unique Next Steps

In Chapter 9, we listed some specific next steps that could be the right unique next step for you. I don't know if those steps will cause you to trust Jesus more; the key to a unique next step is that it is a step that causes *you* to have to trust Jesus more. My steps will look different from your steps. Our faith in Jesus is not one-size-fits-all. Some steps will happen inside the church. Most steps will occur outside the church.

If you want to take this seriously, I've got something you can try. Visit caseyross.net and check out the "Faith Resources" section. One of the free resources you can use is "Track Your Steps." It's a resource that will help you look back at the steps that caused you to trust Jesus more.

It will also help you look forward and determine steps you can take in the future that will cause you to trust Jesus more. Maybe the list below will help you as you look for future steps to take.

- speak with gentleness
- lead a Bible study in your church
- express joy in a challenging situation
- give financially to a local nonprofit
- invite someone to your church
- show more self-control in difficult situations
- travel outside of your community to meet needs
- check yourself into rehab to deal with your addiction
- volunteer in your church

- forgive the person who hurt you
- volunteer in a local nonprofit
- mentor someone in your church
- join a Bible study
- surprise someone by serving them
- help others experience peace
- make your grandchild feel loved
- ask someone to help you better understand the Bible
- ask someone to mentor you
- apply the Bible in ways that cause your faith in Jesus to grow
- travel outside of your country to help others start and grow their faith in Jesus
- eat dinner regularly with your family
- say "no" to an opportunity you'd typically say "yes" to
- go on a vacation and completely unplug from technology
- start a new relationship
- share with someone why you started your faith in Jesus
- volunteer in a local school
- say something kind to the grocery store worker
- quit your job
- help someone else succeed
- say "no" to something that takes up space on your calendar
- show more love to everyone
- become friends with someone unlike your other friends
- be someone others can trust
- rest
- pay for someone's meal
- ask someone if they want to start their faith in Jesus
- don't sign your kid up for the following sports season
- apologize to the person you hurt
- understand the opinions of someone you disagree with
- show love to someone very different from you
- pray with your family every night

- have a meaningful conversation with someone
- pray for someone you do not like
- do a chore at your house that someone else is supposed to do
- hug someone just because
- leave a large tip for the person helping you at a restaurant
- sell something you own and give the money away
- study the Bible by yourself
- say an encouraging word to a stranger
- give up a parking space close to the store
- say "yes" to an opportunity you'd typically say "no" to
- pray out loud in front of others
- do less
- attend church regularly
- ask for forgiveness from someone you hurt
- do something you've never done before
- support a local business
- acknowledge a secret from your past
- ask people if they need anything
- tell that person how they hurt you in the past
- share with someone how Jesus has proven trustworthy in your life
- accept someone very different than you
- verbally encourage someone you don't know
- find out how someone is doing
- put up with someone you find difficult
- show honor to every person you encounter
- serve someone in need
- invite someone you don't usually spend time with to a meal
- carry someone's worry with them
- care for someone who is not easy to care for
- warmly say "hi" to everyone you encounter
- plant a church

There are free resources for you and your friends at caseyross.net. I hope these tools help you develop a habit of taking steps that cause you to trust Jesus more.

Appendix 2: For Church Leaders

I'm one of you. I love the church. I want the best for people. I want Christians to experience what is theirs: being a new creation, being filled with the Holy Spirit, the fruit of the Spirit, leading others to start their faith in Jesus, trusting Jesus more and more, etc., yet I don't see it consistently in Christian's lives.

For decades, I've planned ministries, written curricula, developed new ministries, executed strategies, met with consultants and other pastors, prayed, etc. All the things you do. And I've seen God do many amazing things in people's lives. Jesus established the church to reach the world. The church works!

What I've seen the most, though, is the same-old-same-old: Christians who attend church sometimes. Christians who feel "high" on God after a mission trip or a worship experience eventually return to being like everyone else. Why is there often very little or no difference between someone who is not a Christian and a Christian who has the Spirit of God in them?

I'm tired of people jumping from church to church and trend to trend, chasing "deep" faith. I'm tired of people complaining about the church and what it offers and does not offer.

I'm tired of churches chasing peoples' expectations. I'm tired of churches not changing their strategy to reach the changing world around them. I'm tired of churches acting like they hold the secret to someone's faith. A person's faith in Jesus is their faith. Their faith is their responsibility, not ours or the churches.

The answer is not to get mad at people or the church. The answer is not to give up. I believe the answer is to do things differently. That is the only way we will see different results.

Below are some steps your church can take to maybe, just maybe, see Christians live their lives and live out their faith in ways that influences their community toward faith in Jesus. I do think it's possible.

STEP: BREAK PEOPLE OF THE HABIT OF DEPENDING ON YOU AND THE CHURCH FOR THEIR FAITH

The church should play an important role in a Christian's life and faith, but Christians should play a more important role in the church. The church is not for the people. The people are for the church.

Reduce the number of *hows* your church offers. The *hows* keep people depending on your church. Yes, you need to provide some *hows*. Those are the ways you teach and empower people to live their faith in their community. Keep the number of *hows* you offer to a minimum. Only provide the essential *hows* that lead people to take steps to trust Jesus more.

At Local Church, where I am currently on staff, our *hows* are Sunday worship services, Bible studies, and mentoring. That's it. All three of these things emphasize applying the Bible in ways that cause you to take steps to trust Jesus more.

Here is the list of *hows* from chapter eight:

- small groups
- church membership

- financial giving
- confession
- volunteering
- confirmation classes
- mission trips
- memorized prayers
- baptism
- church retreats
- Sunday school
- accountability groups
- nights of worship
- prayer meetings
- communion
- women's ministries
- vacation Bible school
- revival services
- infant baptism
- outreach night
- Bible studies
- community groups
- first communion
- membership classes
- men's ministries
- mentoring
- catechism classes

Stop doing some of the things you do. How many items should you stop doing? Stop doing enough to get your people's attention that you are doing things differently because you want different results in their faith...and enough to make a difference and cause people to own their faith in Jesus.

STEP: LEAD PEOPLE NOT TO SEEK THE SHALLOW END

Christians pray for peaceful, uncomplicated lives. The goal is to have a fear-free life they can manage. I call this the shallow end. It's the desire to have both feet touching the bottom, so there is no need to trust Jesus.

The shallow end, or the illusion of the shallow end, is dangerous for the people in your church. Pastor, author, and speaker Mark Sayers writes, "Christian leadership is leading people into growth so that they may grow in Christlikeness. Growth, however, involves understanding that discomfort and pain are part of life and can be used by God to grow us. As we have learned, unhealthy individuals and systems make comfort and ease their highest value and thus do everything to avoid discomfort and pain. The choice to prioritize comfort, ease, and good feelings above growth is the choice to embrace and accept personal, spiritual, and emotional immaturity."[33]

Instead of leading your people to seek something that can stunt their spiritual growth, lead them not to be fearful of the uncomfortable times in life. Help them even create uncomfortable times when they must trust Jesus. Disciple your people to know how to grow their faith in the difficult times when their feet do not touch the bottom.

STEP: DECIDE WHAT YOUR CHURCH CAN UNIQUELY OFFER TO YOUR COMMUNITY

I believe all churches have the same answer to this step. I think the one thing every church can uniquely contribute to their community is faith in Jesus. The church can help people start and grow their faith in Jesus.

I don't believe the church uniquely offers community, friendships, food or clothing pantries, Biblical knowledge, accountability, statements on current events, etc., to their community. Other groups can provide those things. Jesus established the church to take his Gospel to the world. That is what we should do.

If you dare to take this step, you must fight to stay clear and focused. You will always be tempted to provide more to your people. Don't do it. Provide one thing: faith in Jesus.

STEP: LEAD PEOPLE TO TAKE UNIQUE NEXT STEPS THAT CAUSE THEM TO TRUST JESUS MORE

Empower your people to live out their faith Monday through Saturday, away from the church.

Expect them to live out their faith Monday through Saturday away from the church.

Make Monday through Saturday far more significant than Sunday. Make Sunday their launch pad, marching orders, strategic plan, fuel, inspiration, and safe place for Monday through Saturday.

Lead them to take steps through your preaching, communication, social media, the few *hows* you offer, etc.

MAYBE I CAN HELP

I love the church. And I'd love to help you and your church. If you think I could help your church take steps forward, visit caseyross.net to contact me. Let's schedule a 30-minute phone call to discuss your situation and setting. If I can help beyond that, I'd love to Zoom, fly, or drive in to work with you and your church.

There are also free resources for church leaders and churches at caseyross.net.

Thank You

Julie, Bennett, Canon, and Teague. You challenge and encourage me to take steps to trust Jesus more and more. And I have watched each of you take steps to trust Jesus more. I love you.

Chris Emmitt, Brian Haas, Nathan Castleberry, Frank Bealer, Mandi Holcombe, and the Local Church Staff. You allowed me to dream about how adults can genuinely grow their faith in Jesus, and we're doing something different.

Paul McQuaid. You were the first person to ask to read this book. You read it before most people knew I was writing it, and you made it much better.

Andy Stanley and my friends at North Point. I spent 15 years in this ministry. To say you influenced me is the understatement of my life. I am forever grateful for how you made me a better human, husband, dad, friend, boss, leader, manager, and, most importantly, Jesus follower.

Evan McLaughlin. You introduced me to the idea of "This is it?" versus "This is it!" in the context of perspective and attitude. To this day, this is one of my all-time favorite sermons.

Chick-fil-A. Most of this book was written in different Chick-fil-A restaurants. If you know me, you know I'm not kidding. Thanks for the tables, Diet Dr. Pepper, and Frosted Coffees.

Phil Wickham. We've never met, but 95% of this book was written while listening to a playlist I made of all your songs. God focuses me when I hear you sing.

Notes

YOUR COMPLICATED LIFE

1   Definitions come from https://www.merriam-webster.com/dictionary/complicated.

2   I Thought It Was Just Me (but it isn't): Making the Journey from "What Will People Think?" to "I Am Enough." Brené Brown. Avery. 2007. Page 29.

3   Dr Chinwé Williams' definition of anxiety comes from our Instagram Direct Message conversation on February 12, 2022.

4   From the Armchair Expert podcast. https://armchairexpertpod.com/pods/ron-howard aired on October 18, 2021. 1:10:10 to 1:10:15.

YOUR WORDS

5   I Said This You Heard That: How Your Wiring Colors Your Communication. Kathleen Edelman. North Point Ministries, Inc. 2018. Page 13.

6   https://www.dictionary.com/e/s/cringeworthy-english-words/#i-cant-stand-that-word

YOUR ACTIONS

7   https://insight.org/resources/bible/the-pauline-epistles/romans

LIFE IS STEPS

8   Definitions come from https://www.merriam-webster.com/dictionary/complicated.

9   Kierkegaard's Journals and Notebooks, Volume 2, Journals EE-KK, Princeton University Press, 2015, Journal JJ:167. 1843, P. 179.

10 From https://www.physicsclassroom.com/class/newtlaws/Lesson-1/Inertia-and-Mass.

11 Harvard Business Review, July 11, 2019. "10,000 Steps A Day – Or Fewer" by Steve Calechman. https://www.health.harvard.edu/blog/10000-steps-a-day-or-fewer-2019071117305

12 Harvard Business Review, July 11, 2019. "10,000 Steps A Day – Or Fewer" by Steve Calechman. https://www.health.harvard.edu/blog/10000-steps-a-day-or-fewer-2019071117305

13 Quote from September 12, 1962. Martin Luther King, Jr. gave a speech at the Park-Sheraton Hotel in New York City, NY to commemorate the centennial of the Preliminary Emancipation Proclamation.

WHAT IS FAITH?

14 Plan B: Further Thoughts On Faith. Anne Lamott. New York: Riverhead. 2006. Page 257.

15 Emotional Healthy Discipleship. Peter Scazzero. Zondervan. 2021. Page 61.

16 Soul Searching: The Religious and Spiritual Lives of American Teenagers. Christian Smith and Melinda Lundquist Denton. Oxford University Press. New York. 2005.

17 Three specific statements come from Chris Emmitt, Senior Pastor of Local Church based in Forsyth County, Georgia.

18 I learned "God loved," "God gave," "we believe," and "we receive" from Andy Stanley, pastor, writer, speaker, and Founder of North Point Ministries.

19 The 7 Habits of Highly Effective People: 30th Anniversary Edition. Stephen R. Covey. Simon & Schuster. New York. 2020. Page 49.

20 Emotional Healthy Discipleship. Peter Scazzero. Zondervan. 2021. Page 159.

THIS IS IT? (WHEN LIFE AND FAITH FEEL DISAPPOINTING)

21 Peter Bregman, Harvard Business Review - The Problem with High Expectations, February 23, 2012 https://hbr.org/2012/02/the-problem-with-high-expectat.html

22 The Knowledge of the Holy. Aiden Wilson Tozer. HarperCollins. 1961. Page 1.

23 The Knowledge of the Holy. Aiden Wilson Tozer. HarperCollins. 1961. Page 8.

THE CHURCH AND YOUR "THIS IS IT?" FAITH

24 The Grace of God. Andy Stanley. Thomas Nelson; 8/14/11 edition (September 12, 2011). Page 196.

25 All quotes from George Patton's estate's website http://generalpatton.com/quotes/.

26 Quote from Ian Simkins' Instagram account @iansimkins on May 11, 2022.

FAITH IS STEPS (AND IT TAKES ONE STEP)

27 Wholehearted Faith. Rachel Held Evans and Jeff Chu. HarperOne; 2021. Page 34.

28 A Non-Anxious Presence: How a Changing and Complex World will Create a Remnant of Renewed Christian Leaders. Mark Sayers. Moody Publishers; 2022. Pages 103-104.

FAITH CELEBRATED IN THE BIBLE

29 Andy Stanley. "Creating a Great Staff Culture – Andy Stanley." Dallas Theological Seminary. YouTube. February 15, 2019. 37:22 – 37:40. https://www.youtube.com/watch?v=OMfjiXjOpTg&t=2245s

30 The Grace Of God: The Gift We Don't Deserve, The Love We Can't Believe. Andy Stanley. Thomas Nelson, 8/14/11 Edition. Pages 24-25.

EVERYBODY'S WATCHING

31 Definition comes from https://www.merriam-webster.com/dictionary/influence.

32 Not In It To Win It: Why Choosing Sides Sidelines The Church. Andy Stanley. Zondervan. 2022. Pages 171 – 172.

33 A Non-Anxious Presence: How a Changing and Complex World will Create a Remnant of
Renewed Christian Leaders. Mark Sayers. Moody Publishers; 2022. Page 111.

About the Author

As a leader and pastor, Casey has not seen it all, but he has seen a lot. He is currently on staff with Local Church, where he creates new ways to help adults trust Jesus more and leads their strategy to start 20 churches in 10 years. He spent 15 years at North Point Ministries: planting a Strategic Partner church, managing operations at their fastest-growing campus at that time, consulting churches around the world, and leading operations at their largest campus. He has written for North Point Ministries, Lifeway, and many other projects.

Casey is a loyal fan of Atlanta sports teams, appreciates a good sneaker game, visits Hilton Head Island as much as possible, and loves Chick-fil-A probably too much. His favorite thing is his family. He and his wife, Julie, have three kids and live in Atlanta.

You can connect with me on:

- https://www.caseyross.net
- https://twitter.com/caseyross
- https://www.facebook.com/caseymross
- https://www.instagram.com/caseyross

Subscribe to my newsletter:

- https://www.caseyross.net